The Creative Writing Handbook

Jay Amberg and Mark Larson

GoodYearBooks
An Imprint of ScottForesman
A Division of HarperCollins*Publishers*

Cover Illustration by Mark Chickinelli

Book Design by The Parker Group

GoodYearBooks are available for every basic curriculum subject plus many enrichment areas. For more Good Year Books, contact your local bookseller or educational dealer. For a complete catalog, please write:

GoodYearBooks
Scott, Foresman and Company
1900 East Lake Avenue
Glenview, Illinois 60025

ISBN 0-673-36013-X

9 RRD 99 98

TABLE OF CONTENTS

Step One: Prewriting • Exploring the Idea • Energizing
Memory • Sensory Memories • Thematic Thoughts

Step Two: Composing • Creating a Draft

Step Three: Revising • Creating Vivid Openings • Effective
Openings by Professional Writers• Transitions • Peer Editing
• Peer Response Activity • Writing the Final Draft
• Proofreading

Step One: Prewriting • Exploring the Idea • Brainstorming

Step Two: Composing • Creating a Draft

Step Three: Revising • Expanding Sensory Details • Sensory
Details by Professional Writers •Creating Endings
• Transitions • Peer Editing • Peer Response Activity
• Writing the Final Draft • Proofreading

Perfecting a Narrative   56

Step One: Prewriting • Exploring the Idea
• Brainstorming

Step Two: Composing • Creating a Draft of a Narrative

Step Three: Revising • Understanding Your Audience
• Editing Activity • Vivid Language by Professional
Writers • Sentence Combining • Transitions • Peer
Editing • Writing the Final Draft • Proofreading

Creating a Short Story   81

Step One: Prewriting • Point of View • Short Story
Structure • Characterization • Exploring Ideas
• Brainstorming

Step Two: Composing • Creating a Draft of a
Short Story

Step Three: Revising • Peer Response Activity • Short
Story Editing • Writing a Final Draft • Proofreading

Introduction

Can you remember what your first day of school was like? Do certain smells remind you of the summertime? Have you ever seen something unusual and then told your friends about it later? Can you close your eyes and picture a place that is special to you? If you answered yes to these questions, then you are already a writer. You already possess the skills to write your own original stories and poems.

We wrote the *Creative Writing Handbook* with the belief that all young writers are inherently creative. You simply need a framework and a few valuable tools to guide you in developing your own natural talent. Think, then, of this handbook as a tool kit. You can use it to build an entire creative writing project or to fix specific writing problems.

This handbook will provide you with all the materials you need to develop as a creative writer. You can, therefore, use the handbook either as a complete guide for your own personal creative writing course or as the common text for a classroom or workshop of fellow writers. Furthermore, this handbook may be used by you independently or under the guidance of a teacher, parent, tutor, or other adult.

The handbook consists of five instructional units—three on narrative writing, one on fiction writing, and one on poetry. The emphasis on narrative writing—non-fictional accounts of personal experiences—stems from our years of working with young writers. We have found that once you have learned through narrative writing to find a voice, set scenes, describe people, use sensory details, edit prose, and so forth, you can then sharpen these skills while doing fictional and poetic writing.

Each of the five instructional units presents:

- An overview
- A step-by-step writing process
- A related example of professional writing
- Related examples of student writing

- Prewriting activities to help you find and focus ideas
- Clear drafting directions
- Excerpts and quotations from famous authors
- Editing activities to help you sharpen your skills and polish your writing

All of the *Creative Writing Handbook's* instructional units are self-contained. This means you can choose to learn about narrative writing without going on to units on fiction or poetry. Or, you can use the poetry writing unit separately from the other units. Each of the prewriting and editing activities can also be used individually. Most of the activities can be completed in about 30 minutes. These activities will enable you to develop writing skills that will make all of your writing—not just your creative writing efforts—more vivid and interesting.

In addition to these five instructional units, some support materials are included in the back of the handbook. The *Writer's Supplement* provides information you need for effective proofreading. A *Glossary* defines a number of writing terms printed in boldface type and used throughout the handbook.

As you progress through the materials in the handbook, we strongly recommend that you keep a writer's journal. The journal will provide a place for you to jot down ideas and images during the pre-writing activities. It will also allow you to generate a host of ideas for school writing assignments. Journal writing often enables you to discover and strengthen your own voice in writing and to understand better the differences between public and private writing. Some guidelines for journal writing appear on pages 10-13 of this handbook.

Finally, for those of you working through this book with other young writers, peer editing sheets are provided in each unit to support the elements examined in that particular unit. Early peer editing sheets help you become comfortable with the editing process itself; later sheets challenge you to provide increasingly effective advice.

Good luck, and good writing.

The Writer's Notebook

A writer learns to write by writing. And, perhaps the best way to make writing a habit is to keep a writer's notebook or journal. Through journal writing you will begin to discover a personal writing voice. You'll start to write more fluidly. Your writing will remind you of everyday speech, but it will be clearer and more forceful.

We will ask you to write descriptions and responses in your notebook to improve your writing skills, but also to provide opportunities for you to learn about yourself. Indeed, journal writing *is* writing to learn, writing to discover. Keeping a record of your life will allow you to rethink your actions and reactions. As you look back over your entries, you'll realize that some of your observations will prove to be insightful, while others will later seem ordinary, maybe even foolish. For example, one of us, as a student, wrote in a journal one summer,

Man has conquered the moon. Last night, when I was walking around and realizing the astronauts were at that very moment landing on the lunar surface, I could not help smiling. I don't know why it moves me so deeply, but it does. Now all there is to do is hope for their safe return—Armstrong, Aldrin, and Collins.

But other entries that summer were much sillier—news about baseball games and onion soup.

Filling in blank pages with writing will also seem much less frightening when you have had numerous opportunities to express yourself, free from correction and judgment. You can take chances with what you write in your notebook. Mistakes are all right because you are exploring ideas, and errors are sometimes part of that process. Recording your thoughts in your notebook allows you to sift and sort, to revise and rewrite.

A writer's notebook naturally includes errors and other problems, but finished pieces of writing—public writing like the narratives, stories, and poems included in this handbook—should be free from mistakes. Through writing in your notebook and writing polished narratives, stories, and poems, you'll come to understand the differences between *private personal writing* and *public creative writing*.

The Notebook Assignment

Use a separate notebook for your writer's journal. Any spiral notebook not used for school or another purpose will do. Hardcover copybooks work even better because they are durable.

As you go through the units in *The Creative Writing Handbook*, jot down your notes and ideas in your writer's notebook. But also write regularly on your own. Write every day if you can. As you get into it, the writing will become easier and more natural. In fact, you will probably find that you have a lot to say.

Still, you may not always know what you want to write about. In case you get stuck, on the next page are some writing topics you can use to get started again.

Journal Topics

best classes
worst classes
extracurricular activities
favorite foods
weekend plans
favorite TV shows
rock concerts
scary experiments
embarrassing moments
favorite athletes
favorite performers
great adventures
parents
siblings
relatives
enemies
heroes
teachers
hobbies
vacations
parties
pets
fights
life's lessons
anger
friends
hatred
important dates
memories
relationships
workouts
politics
problems
observations
anecdotes
lyrics
revenge

ideas
destiny
feelings
dreams
ignorance
knowledge
humor
excitement
regret
secret fantasies
pet peeves
favorite movies
difficult books
new fashions
major crushes
future plans
controversial news
recent arguments
funny incidents
essential needs
holidays
stars
diets
decisions
love
education
schoolwork
hometown
weather
nature
summer
shopping
music
gossip
poetry
technology
unforgettable moments

Unit 1: Beginning a Narrative

Let's start with narrative writing, which can be defined as a story, an orderly personal account of an experience or event. You do not have to go beyond your own experience to write narratives, but you do have to organize the material and present it vividly to your readers.

You will learn the basics of good writing as you work through the three narrative writing units in this handbook. Each of the narrative writing units will provide you with a general topic that serves as both a framework and a starting point for your writing.

The first narrative writing topic is **Early School Experience**. Since much of narrative writing depends on energizing your memory, we suggest that you begin with this topic because everyone has some kind of shared school experiences. Each of your memories of school experiences will help you remember others. Indeed, you probably have more memories stored in the "file cabinets" of your mind than you may at first realize.

In this first unit, you will learn to:

• Create openings that both catch a reader's interest and focus attention on the experience to be described.
• Use sensory details to set scenes and describe people, places, and objects.
• Do peer editing.
• Use transitions to bridge the gaps from detail to detail and scene to scene.
• Correct mechanical errors.

Step One: Prewriting

Exploring the Idea

You are going to write about experiences you had during your first few years in school. But before you start to write, we would like you to read examples from a professional writer and two young writers like yourself.

Begin with a scene from Harper Lee's famous novel *To Kill a Mockingbird* that appears on the following pages. The narrator, Scout Finch, is describing what happened on the afternoon of her first day in first grade. Miss Caroline is a new teacher. Pay particular attention to the description of Burris Ewell, the boy who has the confrontation with Miss Caroline.

...a sudden shriek shattered my resentments. I looked up to see Miss Caroline standing in the middle of the room, sheer horror flooding her face. Apparently she had revived enough to persevere in her profession.

"It's alive!" she screamed.

The male population of the class rushed as one to her assistance. Lord, I thought, she's scared of a mouse. Little Chuck Little, whose patience with all living things was phenomenal, said, "Which way did he go, Miss Caroline? Tell us which way he went, quick! D.C.—" he turned to a boy behind him—"D.C., shut the door and we'll catch him. Quick ma'am, where'd he go?"

Miss Caroline pointed a shaking finger not at the floor nor at a desk, but to a hulking individual unknown to me. Little Chuck's face contracted and he said gently, "You mean him, ma'am? Yessum, he's alive. Did he scare you some way?"

Miss Caroline said desperately, "I was just walking by when it crawled out of his hair…just crawled out his hair—"…

…The cootie's host showed not the faintest interest in the furor he had wrought. He searched the scalp above his forehead, located his guest and pinched it between his thumb and forefinger.

Miss Caroline watched the process in horrid fascination. Little Chuck brought water in a paper cup, and she drank it gratefully. Finally she found her voice. "What is your name, son?" she asked softly.

The boy blinked. "Who, me?" Miss Caroline nodded.

"Burris Ewell."

Miss Caroline inspected her roll-book. "I have a Ewell here, but I don't have a first name … would you spell your first name for me?"

"Don't know how. They call me Burris't home."

"Well, Burris," Miss Caroline said, "I think we'd better excuse you for the rest of the afternoon. I want you to go home and wash your hair."

From her desk she produced a thick volume, leafed

through its pages, and read for a moment. "A good home remedy for—Burris, I want you to go home and wash your hair...."

...The boy stood up. He was the filthiest human I had ever seen. His neck was dark gray, the backs of his hands were rusty, and his fingernails were black deep into the quick. He peered at Miss Caroline from a fist-sized clean space on his face...

"And Burris," said Miss Caroline, "please bathe yourself before you come back tomorrow."

The boy laughed rudely. "You ain't sendin' me home, missus. I was on the verge of leavin'—I done done my time for this year."

Miss Caroline looked puzzled. "What do you mean by that?"

The boy did not answer. He gave a short, contemptuous snort.

One of the elderly members of the class answered her: "He's one of the Ewells, ma'am. Whole school's full of 'em. They come first day every year and then leave. The truant lady gets 'em here 'cause she threatens 'em with the sheriff, but she's give up tryin' to hold 'em. She reckons she's carried out the law just gettin' their names on the roll and runnin' 'em here the first day. You're supposed to mark 'em absent the rest of the year..."

"But what about their parents?" asked Miss Caroline, in genuine concern.

"But what about their parents?" asked Miss Caroline, in genuine concern.

"Ain't got no mother," was the answer, "and their paw's right contentious."

Burris Ewell was flattered by the recital. "Been comin' to the first day o' the first grade fer three year now," he said expansively. "Reckon if I'm smart this year they'll promote me to the second...."

Miss Caroline said, "Sit back down, please, Burris," and the moment she said it I knew she had made a serious mistake. The boy's condescension flashed to anger.

"You try and make me, missus."

Little Chuck Little got to his feet. "Let him go, ma'am," he said. "He's a mean one, a hard-down mean one. He's liable to start somethin', and there's some little folks here."

He was among the most diminutive of men, but when Burris Ewell turned toward him, Little Chuck's right hand went to his pocket. "Watch your step, Burris," he said. "I'd soon's kill you as look at you. Now go home."

Burris seemed to be afraid of a child half his height, and Miss Caroline took advantage of his indecision: "Burris, go home. If you don't, I'll call the principal," she said. "I'll have to report this, anyway."

The boy snorted and slouched leisurely to the door.

Here is a list of questions to help you think about the scene. Write the answers to these questions in your writer's notebook.

1. What did Burris Ewell look like? How does Lee describe him?

2. How does Burris Ewell kill the cootie? Why is this memorable?

3. How do you think that you and your first grade classmates would have reacted to Burris and the "cootie incident"?

4. What do you remember about your teachers in kindergarten (first grade)?

5. Who were the most memorable students in your kindergarten (first grade) classes? What were these students like?

Next, read the excerpt from the narrative below by a young student writer named Molly Boren. Molly wrote this when she was an eighth-grader. Pay particular attention to the description of Mrs. Tutulo and the craft projects.

Memories of Kindergarten

Looking around the classroom, I recognized a few faces: Beth MacDonald, who lived down the street; Curtis Denham, who had been in my play group; and, of course, Abbie, my sister. We're twins. "We don't look much alike because we're fraternal," we always explain. This was our first day of kindergarten and I guess I was lucky. I think I had a feeling of security because Abbie's sometimes-all-too-familiar face was around.

I don't even remember my mother leaving me that day, like so many people seem to. I just felt a little intimidated by all the papers and books being passed around the class and by the strict authority in Mrs. Tutulo's voice.

Mrs. Tutulo was tall and lanky and had pale, narrow lips that always seemed to lie limply across her thin face in a vacant expression. She was about fifty at the time. Her cropped hair was light gray and streaked with wisps of white and black and she sported an impressive Roman nose.

I don't really recall learning anything in kindergarten. Nothing about reading, writing, or arithmetic, I mean. But I think I got something out of Mrs. Tutulo's class that year that was a little more important that I'll benefit from for the rest of my life. I think it was a feeling of comfort and belonging, an idea that I was a part of a group.

We always seemed to be working on little craft projects like birdfeeders made out of peanut butter and birdseed and paper baskets filled with candy for the residents of Bowling Green Manor, the nursing home down the street. I distinctly remember making Christmas tree ornaments out of paper cups and tin foil. They looked like little silver bells and they still hang from our tree at Christmas time....

... After our kindergarten year was over, Abbie and I were moved to a different school in town. We didn't see most of our friends from Mrs. Tutulo's class much at all

during the rest of elementary school, so we made new friends at our new school. A few years later, Mrs. Tutulo died of lung cancer. I hadn't talked to her in more than five years.

Sometimes it seems to me that all of the innocence and playfulness has gone out of the world. But when Christmas rolls around, and we put an evergreen in our family room, and decorate it with electric lights and shimmering icicles and two little silver bells made out of paper cups and tin foil, I remember how everything was good and honest then and I feel a little better.

Molly Boren

Here are some questions to help you think about Molly's narrative. Write the answers to these questions in your writer's notebook.

1. What did Mrs. Tutulo look like? Does she sound like someone you would want as a teacher?
2. In what ways does this narrative remind you of your first-grade class?
3. How do the two silver bells make Molly feel now? Why? What special souvenirs do you have that remind you of kindergarten and first grade?

Here is another student's narrative. Suzanne Goh was in eighth grade when she wrote about meeting a boy and their going to the first day of kindergarten together. Pay particular attention to Suzanne's descriptions of their meeting and of what happened on her porch.

Will You Marry Me?

One evening in late spring, when I was four and my sister seven, my mother took the two of us for a tricycle and Big Wheel ride around the neighborhood. In a court that turned off from our street, we saw two little boys about our age riding their bikes around their cozy ranch style house. We rode up to their driveway very slowly because I was still at the age of experimenting with the Big Wheel and had a hard time keeping the front wheel moving continuously. My mother struck up a friendly conversation with the boys' mother when we finally got there. That was how I met my very special childhood playmate.

At four years of age, there was very little for a girl to do besides go to pre-school and play on the backyard swing set; therefore, much of my time was spent playing with my new friend Mikey Ruman. Mikey was a short little four year old with soft, milky blonde hair and twinkling blue eyes. We spent those long afternoons with each other on the swing set, in a small inflatable pool, or just sitting on the porch licking popsicles that turned our tongues red, purple, or blue. Our conversation was very limited because there seemed to be no need for it. Mikey and I sat comfortably in each other's quiet presence. We didn't care much about what we did as long as we had someone with which to do it, and Mikey lived just around the corner and was a fine playmate for me.

It was the cool, sunny morning of the first day of kindergarten for Mikey and me. We sat in our new school clothes on my front porch and waited in silence for our parents to walk us to school. I wore my light pink pinstriped sundress with my matching "Buster-Brown" sandals and a little ribbon tied in my long black hair. Mikey had on a miniature men's suit that had a tiny navy bow tie and navy corduroy pants. On his feet were little penny loafers with shiny 1980 pennies tucked into the little pockets. We sat there for a long time in silence when Mikey turned to me and whispered, "Will you marry me?" Unstartled and with the confidence and irrational reasoning of an adult I replied, "I can't because you're not Chinese.'" Tears began streaming down Mikey's soft rosy little face, but he still looked at me steadily through his shining blue eyes. Just as my mom walked out of the house to take us to school, I leaned over and gave Mikey a soft peck on the cheek, and he stopped crying.

The two of us walked to and from school together until second grade. That was when we began noticing the difference between boys and girls, and unfortunately placed our friendship aside. It was the end of our childhood bliss and our innocence about true love. It was the end of our simple world and the beginning of reality.

Suzanne Goh

Here are some questions to help you think about Suzanne's narrative. Write your answers to these questions in your notebook.

1. What do the two children do together? What did you do with your friends when you were four or five?

2. What clothes did the children wear on their first day of school? Why? What was your favorite outfit when you were young?

3. What lesson did Suzanne learn in this narrative? Did you have a similar experience when you were young?

Energizing Memory

Begin to think about which of your early school experiences you can turn into a lively narrative. A minute or so of "quiet time" for reflection can go a long way towards getting the ball rolling. Journey back in time for a bit. Look to your own kindergarten (or first-grade) classroom. Picture yourself as a young child and your surroundings.

Now write for a minute or two in your notebook. Jot down whatever comes into your mind. This will ensure that you will have *something* to say about the topic.

Next, choose from among the following "starters" those topics and questions that will best energize your memory. Sometimes it helps to begin with physical— that is, **sensory**—details. Other times it is more useful to think in terms of **themes**, key ideas that stand out in your mind.

Sensory Memories

• What did your kindergarten classroom look like?
• What sounds do you remember hearing in your kindergarten room?

- What did you wear in kindergarten? How did the other kindergartners dress?
- What did your kindergarten teacher look like?

Thematic Thoughts

Culture Shock

- What can you remember about your first day of kindergarten (first grade)?
- How did you feel when you realized that you were on your own?

The Daily Grind

- What was done every day in kindergarten (first grade)? What was your favorite part of the day? Why?

The Learning Curve

- How did you learn to read? What were your favorite books? What do you remember about learning to write?

Young Love

- Did you have a crush on anyone in your class? Who? Why?
- How did you let him or her know?

Crime and Punishment

- Did you ever get in any trouble? What did you do?

Going Home Again

- Have you ever returned to your kindergarten (first grade) classroom? How did the classroom look to you?

Step Two: Composing

Creating a Draft

Now write a draft of your narrative. The length of narratives will always vary, but a good average length is one-and-a-half to three pages. Shorter narratives tend to lack description, and longer narratives are often wordy.

You can write about one specific experience, as Harper Lee did in *To Kill a Mockingbird*, or about a number of experiences in a particular grade. A narrative about a single experience should probably be organized **chronologically**—in the order that the event occurred. A narrative about a series of related experiences should probably be organized by ideas—the classroom, the teacher, other students, and so forth.

The key point here is to get the *entire* narrative down on paper. The novelist John Steinbeck wrote, "'Write freely and as rapidly as possible and throw the whole thing on paper. Never correct or rewrite until the whole thing is down." Correct grammar, punctuation, and mechanics are important, of course, but there will be an opportunity later to edit and proofread your draft. For now, your goal is a workable draft.

Don't be too hard on yourself. First, let the ideas flow. One way to do this is to write, nonstop, for a certain time period—say, five or ten minutes. Write lists, sentences, paragraphs—write anything. It is always easier to discard unnecessary details than to create new ones later.

Here is some advice from well-known, published writers. We are including the quotes to remind you that writing is not "easy" even for professional writers. Read each of the quotations. Then, write down in your notebook the quote that you most want to remember.

Experience has shown me that there are no miracles in writing. The only thing that produces good writing is hard work.
—Isaac Bashevis Singer

I wanted to be a writer when I was in sixth grade—of course I wanted to be one without working at it.
—Joseph Heller

There is no mechanical way to get the writing done, no short cut. The young writer would be a fool to follow a theory. Teach yourself by your own mistakes; people learn only by error.
—William Faulkner

At the time of writing, I don't write for my friends or myself, either; I write for "it," the pleasure of "it."
—Eudora Welty

I always know the ending; that's where I start.
—Toni Morrison

Now, keeping Steinbeck's advice in mind, write the draft of your early school narrative in your notebook.

Step Three: Revising

Creating Vivid Openings

Let's begin the process of revision by examining and editing your opening. Openings should do two things: catch a reader's interest and focus the attention on the topic of the narrative. As you complete the following activity, you will discover that you can spot a good opening when you read one. This should help you to edit your own openings with confidence.

Remember—Narrative openings should do two things: Catch the reader's interest and focus the reader's attention on the topic of the narrative.

Examine each of the following openings to students' narratives about early school experiences. Decide if each opening both catches your interest and informs you about the topic of the narrative.

A. " 'Sherel has cooties' was a normal playground howl in second grade."

Does this opening interest you? Explain.

_____

_____

B. "One especially gloomy Monday morning in third grade, my mother cruelly reminded me that I had forgotten to cut out a current events article for my class's weekly current events day."

Does this opening interest you? Explain.

_____

_____

What will this narrative be about?

_____

_____

C. "I sat in the second to last row in Miss Mulligan's classroom. My eyes were glued not on the minute hand of the clock, as were everyone else's, but rather on a boy two rows to my right and three seats up."

Does this opening interest you? Explain.

_____

_____

What will this narrative be about?

_____

_____

_____

_____

Effective Openings by Professional Writers

You may at this point wish to read some examples of openings by professional writers. Below is the famous opening to Charles Dickens's novel *A Tale of Two Cities*.

It was the best of times, it was the worst of times, it was the age of wisdom, it was the age of foolishness, it was the epoch of belief, it was the epoch of incredulity, it was the season of Light, it was the season of Darkness, it was the spring of hope, it was the winter of despair, we had everything before us, we had nothing before us, we were all going direct to Heaven, we were all going direct the other way....

1. Does this opening catch your interest? Explain.

_____

_____

_____

2. Does this opening focus your attention on what the book will be about? Explain.

_____

_____

_____

Here are references to seven more examples of good narrative openings by professional writers that you may want to look up and read.

1. James Herriot's *All Creatures Great and Small*
Chapter One: first page (birthing a calf)
2. S.E. Hinton's *The Outsiders*
Chapter One: first page (leaving the theater)
3. Garrison Keillor's *We Are Still Married*
"The Babe": paragraphs 1-3 (turning thirteen)
4. Jean Shepherd's "Endless Streetcar Ride into the Night"
Paragraphs 1 and 2 (the blind date)
5. E.B. White's "Once More to the Lake"
Paragraph 1 (summer of 1904)
6. Paul Zindel's *The Pigman*
Chapter One: paragraphs 1 and 2 (the bathroom bomber)

A. Now, write your opening sentence here.

_____

_____

_____

1. Will your opening interest your readers?

_____

2. Does your opening suggest to your readers what your narrative will be about?_____

B. Rewrite your opening, making any necessary changes.

_____

_____

_____

_____

Transitions

Transitions are words or phrases that provide your readers with bridges from point to point or scene to scene in your writing. Here is a list of simple words and phrases to use as transitions in your writing. As you go back over your draft, use these words to connect your thoughts. Use them to join or sequence sentences or whole paragraphs.

again	finally	secondly
also	first	then
at last	first of all	third(ly)
but	lastly	though
now	of course	too

Peer Editing

Writers often have someone else read what they write before it is published. Nowadays, this process is commonly referred to as **peer editing**. A peer—that is, someone who is your equal—reads your writing and gives you advice about how to improve it. Find someone to be your "editor." He or she might be a friend, classmate, an older brother or sister—anyone interested in writing.

Being a good editor of someone else's work can help you as a writer, too, because it forces you to think more about what makes for good writing. In fact, you will see that your own writing improves as you develop your editing skills. Thus, the editing guides in this book start simply but gradually become more demanding. Early editing worksheets focus on becoming familiar with the editing process itself. They pose questions that all young writers should feel comfortable answering. ("Summarize the piece of writing." "Parts that I liked best were," etc.) Later, the editing guides pose more challenging questions. Each of the editing guides stresses a **stylistic** point. For example, in Unit Two, the peer response sheet requires editors to identify a section that could use more sensory details.

The most obvious benefit of having someone read your writing is that you will like the advice and find it helpful. But even advice you don't like can prove helpful. Here are two possible outcomes of peer editing:

• The advice is obviously insightful; you can use it to improve your drafts.

This is, of course, the best situation. Here you have a chance to evaluate the advice of one reader—your peer editor. This enables you to evaluate your own draft again. Good advice from your peer editor has the added benefit of actually giving you useful suggestions that you can use right away.

• The editor disliked your draft; you wonder if the advice can be useful.

How is peer editing beneficial, if the comments are critical? The misconception here is that having an outside reader is not in and of itself beneficial. There is a good deal more objectivity to a peer editor's outlook than to the writer's. For example, you may suspect that your introductory section is rather boring but be reluctant to admit it. To you, it means going back and rewriting that section. An outside reader does not think about the amount of work involved in "fixing" the opening. He or she only cares if it is interesting.

Regardless of the advice, you should still examine the draft again. Writers are always free to accept or reject suggestions from their peer editors. Keep an open mind about suggestions. Just the practice of going back and re-examining your writing is useful in making you a better writer.

• Remember that through peer editing, you'll get the opportunity to hone your editing and writing skills.

It is easy enough to give advice to others. The hard part is to have to follow through with the advice yourself! The more chances you have to read other writer's drafts and make decisions about them the better. By reading other writers, you begin to see how they "solve" problems—how they begin, how they organize details, how they create interest in what they have to say. Your practice as an editor of someone else's writing will help you also manage your own drafts. Plus, you will have the benefit of being exposed to alternate writing styles and approaches.

Peer Response Activity

Ask your peer editor to read your narrative and answer the following questions about it:

Read the opening section of the narrative and then stop to answer questions 1 and 2. Then finish the narrative and complete the response sheet by answering the questions on a separate piece of paper.

1. Does this opening interest you? Explain. If it does not, suggest a way to make it better.
2. What do you think this narrative will be about?
3. Summarize the narrative in one or two sentences.
4. Finish this statement: Things I liked best were...
5. Complete this statement: Things I would like to know more about were...

Writing the Final Draft

Before writing a **final draft**, read through your narrative carefully, making any changes you think will improve your writing. Think about your peer editor's suggestions. Be sure that your opening gets your readers' attention and lets them know what your narrative is about. Make sure that your descriptions are clear and vivid. See that your transitions lead your readers easily through your narrative. Then, write out a final, public copy of your narrative that can be shared with other people.

Proofreading

In **proofreading**, you check for and correct mechanical errors. Proofreading is the last step you will take before finishing a final, public draft of your writing. After you have made the editorial changes you feel improve your narrative, go back over the piece to correct any mechanical errors. In the *Writer's Supplement* at the end of this handbook, there is a review of English style and usage. Use this information to enable you to proofread your papers with confidence.

Unit 2: Developing a Narrative

The writing topic in this unit is an "Imaginative Childhood Experience." As children, we are naturally imaginative. We love to create games and conjure images that later provide a rich vein of memorable experiences. These memories can be mined not only for narratives but also for poems and short stories. As you write about imaginative childhood activities, you will find that your use of vivid imagery will improve.

In this unit you will learn to:

- Use **sensory imagery** to set scenes and describe people, places, and objects.
- Create clever and lively endings for narratives.
- Expand **sensory details** to involve the reader in the narrative.
- Use transitions to bridge the gaps from detail to detail and scene to scene.
- Edit prose to make writing more concise and persuasive.
- Correct mechanical errors.

Step One: Prewriting

Exploring the Idea

Soon you are going to have the chance to write about imaginative childhood games and experiences. Before you begin to write, you will read examples from a professional writer and a young beginning writer.

Below is another excerpt from Harper Lee's *To Kill a Mockingbird*. The first passage describes the Radley house and suggests how the townspeople, especially the children, react to Boo Radley's presence there. Pay particular attention to the description of the house.

Note the impression the passage leaves on you.

The Radley Place jutted into a sharp curve beyond our house. Walking south, one faced its porch; the sidewalk turned and ran beside the lot. The house was low, was once white with a deep front porch and green shutters, but had long ago darkened to the color of the slate-grey yard around it. Rain-rotted shingles drooped over the eaves of the veranda, oak trees kept the sun away. The remains of a picket drunkenly guarded the front yard—a "swept" yard that was never swept—where johnson grass and rabbit-tobacco grew in abundance.

Inside the house lived a malevolent phantom. People said he existed, but Jem and I had never seen him. People said he went out at night when the moon was down, and peeped in windows. When people's azaleas froze in a cold snap, it was because he had breathed on them. Any stealthy small crimes committed in Maycomb were his work.... The Maycomb school grounds adjoined the back of the Radley lot; from the Radley chickenyard tall pecan trees shook their fruit into the schoolyard, but the nuts lay untouched by the children: Radley pecans would kill you. A baseball hit into the Radley yard was a lost ball and no questions asked.

Children often dare each other to do scary things. In the next scene Dill, Scout's neighbor, is daring Jem, Scout's brother, to go up and physically touch the Radley house. Note especially the verbs Harper Lee uses to show Jem's actions.

Jem stood in thought so long that Dill made a mild concession: "I won't say you ran out on a dare an' I'll swap you The Gray Ghost if you just go up and touch the house."

Jem brightened. "Touch the house, that all?"

Dill nodded.

"Sure that's all, now? I don't want you hollerin' something different the minute I get back."

"Yeah, that's all," said Dill,... "Scout and me's right behind you."

He walked to the corner of the lot, then back again, studying the simple terrain as if deciding how best to effect an entry, frowning and scratching his head.

Then I sneered at him.

Jem threw open the gate and sped to the side of the house, slapped it with his palm and ran back past us, not waiting to see if his foray was successful. Dill and I followed on his heels. Safely on our porch, panting and out of breath, we looked back.

The old house was the same, droopy and sick, but as we stared down the street we thought we saw an inside shutter move. Flick. A tiny, almost invisible movement, and the house was still.

Here is a list of specific questions to help you think about the scenes. Write the answers in your notebook.

1. What did the Radley place look like? What words would you use to describe it?

2. Who lives in the Radley place? What do the children think he is like?

3. What can you tell about Jem from the second passage? Does he remind you of anyone you grew up with?

4. Was there any place in your neighborhood that you avoided? Why?

5. When you were younger, what sorts of things scared you? Did you believe in any phantoms or monsters?

Children also often make up imaginative games to play. Read the narrative "Let's Say" by Molly Boren. Think about the imaginative games that you played with your friends when you were younger. Pay particular attention to the way Cindy talks and to the other girls' reactions.

Let's Say

"Let's say there's this Mrs. Bradshaw," Cindy began. "And she's really rich and snobby and spends all her time going to the country club and drinking spritzers. And she's got this daughter and she decides to get her a nanny so she won't have to bother with her. She puts like an ad in the newspaper or something and this really poor but really nice lady comes in for an interview. She gets the job and works there for a while and then they

find out that the Nice Lady should really have all the Mean Lady's money and stuff and the Mean Lady has to work for her."

She took a breath and looked around the room for our troupe's approval. Sarah, my twin sister, and I beamed toward her with adoration. Cindy was the best. She was six years older than we, but she played with us almost every day. I find that amazing now that I'm older and I look back on those days; those days when Cindy and Jeannie would pile into our concrete-floored, roughly decorated basement with us and we'd drift into one of our pretend worlds. Jeannie was three years older than Sarah and I and a prized member of our basement actors' guild. Sarah and I must have been about five or six then. The four of us thought up anything and everything from "karate woman" to "haunted house" to "princess."

Cindy and Jeannie originated most of the plots. First, one of them would come up with a basic story-line, many times a recycled one. They would loosely explain it to the rest of us between sips of cherry Kool-aid and cheese sandwiches, like Cindy had done this particular time. Then we'd criticize and add details and choose up roles and costumes. As we played, we'd make up dialogue and sometimes even change the whole drama if we got a sudden "let's say" urge....

Molly Boren

Now, answer these questions in your notebook.

1. Is "Let's Say" a good title? Explain.
2. When you were six, would you have liked to play

3. What details remind you of your own "pretend" games?
4. Whom did you or your friends pretend to be?
5. What were the best roles? The worst roles? Did you ever argue over what character you would be?

Brainstorming

Concentrate on your own recollections of childhood games and fantasies. As a warm-up to your brainstorming session, write a brief response to this question in your notebook: "If you could go back in time for just one afternoon to being six years old again, what kind of game or activity would you be sure to play?" Now respond in your notebook to these questions:

Group Fun

• What were your favorite childhood games? Why?
• In your neighborhood did you play any special games you invented yourselves? What were these games like?

Rainy Days and Solitaire

• What kinds of activities were saved only for those days when you were stuck inside on a rainy day?
• What kinds of games did you play by yourself? Were they more or less fun when others tried to play too? Why?

• Did you ever act out your daydreams? Did you have any imaginary "friends"? What were their names? What did you want to be when you grew up?

Dress Up

• Were there any TV shows or movies you acted out? Which ones?
• Did you wear costumes? What kind? Where did you get them?

Spooky Stuff

• When it got dark, what seemed scariest?
• What monsters lurked in your house?
• When you pulled the covers over your head, what were you hiding from?
• Was there anything hiding under your bed? In the closet?
• Were there any scary or "haunted" places in your neighborhood?
• What were they like? How did you avoid them?

Step Two: Composing

Creating a Draft

Now write a draft of your narrative about a childhood activity. The length of the narrative will vary depending upon the time and effort you give the assignment, but a good average length is one to three pages. Shorter narratives tend to lack sensory details.

You can write about any imaginative childhood activity, including neighborhood games, games played alone, role-playing activities, and scary moments. The key is to get the *entire* narrative down on paper. Correct grammar, punctuation, and mechanics matter, but there will be plenty of opportunity later to edit and proofread the draft. For now, the goal is to create a readable draft that can be shared with someone else.

Now, write the draft of your imaginative childhood narrative in your notebook.

Step Three: Revising

The process of revision can sometimes be difficult. Even professional writers are often overwhelmed by the task of revising as well. The professional writers' quotations about revision that appear below suggest just how hard it can be to revise your writing. Read each of the quotations. Then write down in your notebook the quote that you most want to remember.

My reputation for writing quickly and effortlessly notwithstanding, I am strongly in favor of intelligent, even fastidious revision, which is, or certainly should be, an art itself.
—Joyce Carol Oates

Every word is there for a reason, and if not, I cross it out.
—*Jerzy Kosinski*

Generally, I write everything many times over. All my thoughts are second thoughts. And I correct each page a great deal, or rewrite it several times as I go along.
—*Aldous Huxley*

For me, revising is mostly a matter of language and selection. I don't try to change the narrative or the point of view.
—*Gore Vidal*

For me it's mostly a question of rewriting. It's part of a constant attempt on my part to make the finished version smooth, to make it seem effortless.
—*James Thurber*

I rewrote the ending to Farewell to Arms, *the last page of it, thirty-nine times before I was satisfied.*
—*Ernest Hemingway*

The revising activities in this unit concentrate on presenting and expanding sensory details. Good narrative writing is generally brimming with these details. **Sensory details** are placed in sentences and phrases in order to form pictures in our minds of what things look, sound, feel, smell, and taste like. They appeal to our senses. They *show* what a person or place looks and sounds like. They help us to understand, for example, exactly what a rabbit's fur feels like or what a freshly baked apple pie smells like or what a scoop of double-fudge chocolate-chip ice cream tastes like.

To see how writers create sensory imagery and learn how to write sensory details, complete the following activity:

Expanding Sensory Details

A. Compare the following sentence to Harper Lee's description of Burris Ewell.

— *The boy was real dirty.*

— *"The boy stood up. He was the filthiest human I had ever seen. His neck was dark gray, the backs of his hands were rusty, and his fingernails were black deep into the quick. He peered at Miss Caroline from a fist-sized clean space on his face."*

Cover up Lee's sensory description of Burris Ewell. Then, close your eyes for a moment and picture him in your mind. Without looking back at the description, answer these questions.

1. What did his hands look like?

_____

_____

2. How big was the clean space on his face?

_____

_____

3. How well does Lee's description create a picture in your mind? Why?

_____

_____

_____

B. Compare the following sentence to Harper Lee's description of the Radley Place.

—*The house was a little broken down.*

—*"The Radley Place jutted into a sharp curve beyond our house.... The house was low, was once white with a deep front porch and green shutters, but had long ago darkened to the color of the slate-grey yard around it. Rain-rotted shingles drooped over the eaves of the veranda, oak trees kept the sun away. The remains of a picket drunkenly guarded the front yard...."*

C. In the first sentence, you are just told the house is broken down, but Harper Lee *shows* you the broken down Radley Place. Notice the verbs that she uses. What does each of these verbs mean?

1. jutted   **2.** drooped   **3.** guarded

Do verbs like these create pictures in your mind? How?

_____

_____

_____

Sensory Details by Professional Writers

At this point you may wish to read some examples of vivid sensory details by professional writers. Below is a passage from Jack London's "To Build a Fire." Notice how London makes us feel the cold along with his main character.

All a man had to do was keep his head, and he was all right. Any man who was a man could travel alone. But it was surprising, the rapidity with which his cheeks and nose were freezing. And he had not thought his fingers could go lifeless in so short a time. Lifeless they were, for he could scarcely make them move together to grip a twig, and they seemed remote from his body and from him. When he touched a twig, he had to look and see whether or not he had hold of it. The wires were pretty well down between him and his finger-ends.

1. What effect is the cold having on his fingers?

_____

_____

2. Predict what will happen next.

_____

_____

_____

Here are references to some more passages, written by professional writers, which stress vivid sensory details.

1. Maya Angelou's *I Know Why the Caged Bird Sings*, "Graduation Day" (preparations for the event)
2. Irwin Shaw's "80 Yard Run" (the locker room scene)
3. Mark Twain's *The Adventures of Huckelberry Finn*, Chapter IX (watching the summer storm)
4. E.B. White's "Once More to the Lake" (storm in the afternoon)

Now, reread your description of the most important person in your narrative. Expand that description in your notebook. Use sensory details. *Show* your readers what the person looks like. Use this new version in your next draft.

Next, reread your description of the setting of your narrative. Expand that description. Use sensory details to describe the setting. *Show* your readers what the setting looks, sounds, and even smells like. Write your improved description and then build it into your next draft.

Creating Endings

Narrative endings should wrap up the story in a lively, clever way.

A. Examine each of the following endings of narratives. Decide if each ending both interests you and wraps up the narrative.

—*Since then, Jeffrey has had dates with many girls. He still does not, though, notice that there are kids who gaze at him from behind.*

1. Does this ending interest you? Explain.

_____

_____

_____

_____

2. What was this narrative probably about?

_____

_____

_____

_____

—*After that our teacher treated everyone with respect, especially Sherel. And for the rest of my years in grammar school, there were only two games the boys played on the playground.*

3. Does this ending interest you? Explain.

_____

_____

4. What was this narrative probably about?

_____

_____

_____

B. Reread the ending to your narrative. How well does your ending wrap up the story?

_____

_____

How clever and lively is your ending?

_____

_____

C. In your notebook, draft a rewrite of the ending of your narrative. Then incorporate it in your next draft.

Transitions

Here is a list of words and phrases to use as transitions and to introduce sensory imagery. As you go back over your draft, use these words and phrases to make the bridges between details and scenes more clear and smooth.

actually	afterward
by the way	for example
for instance	furthermore
however	in other words
in the first place	in the meantime
meanwhile	nevertheless
on the other hand	similarly
yet	

Peer Editing

Here is a peer response activity you can ask your peer editor to complete, on a separate sheet of paper, for the draft of your narrative. Use the responses to re-evaluate your narrative.

Peer Response Activity

1. Summarize the piece of writing in one or two sentences.
2. Complete this statement: Things I liked best were...
3. List the things you would like to know more about.
4. List the most vivid sensory details you recall.
5. Finish this sentence: A section that could use more sensory details was...
6. Evaluate the ending. Does it wrap up the story in a lively?

Writing the Final Draft

Before writing a final draft, read through your narrative carefully, making any changes you think will improve the writing. Review your peer editor's observations and suggestions. Be sure that you have expanded sensory details, especially your descriptions of people and places. See that your transitions lead your readers easily through the narrative. Make sure that your opening and closing are clear, clever, and vivid. Then, write out a final, public copy of your narrative that can be shared with other people.

Proofreading

As a writer, your goal is to communicate clearly with the readers. Make your writing easy to follow. After all, a reader can always choose to read something else. Proofread your narrative to make sure that there are no mistakes that would confuse your readers. Read your narrative aloud so that you can hear where the writing doesn't work. Trust your ear. Use the natural rhythms of speech.

Unit 3: Perfecting a Narrative

The narrative writing topic of this unit is "A Significant Experience." In this unit, you have a much broader choice of what to write about. The key is to choose a subject that is important to you—an event or series of events that influenced you. If you choose an experience significant in your life, you will not only be able to remember the details about it, but you will also bring an enthusiasm to the writing that will involve and affect your readers.

In this unit, you will learn to:

- Choose the "right word" when describing people, places, and objects.
- Develop a sense of audience.
- Use transitions to bridge from detail to detail and scene to scene.
- Combine sentences to make writing flow more smoothly.
- Edit prose to make writing more concise and persuasive.
- Hone editing skills.
- Correct mechanical errors.

Step One: Prewriting

Exploring the Idea

Before you begin to write about a significant experience in your life, you will read examples from a professional writer and a student writer like yourself.

Below is a passage from "Breakfast" by John Steinbeck. This narrative about a chance meeting the narrator had one morning with some people living in poverty presents a seemingly ordinary experience, yet it made a lasting impression. One mark of good narrative writing is the ability to bring routine experiences alive.

Steinbeck enriches the way we look at a simple, everyday event like having breakfast. He lends it a sense of drama and dignity, and, in the process, helps his readers look at it in a new way. Pay particular attention to Steinbeck's sensory descriptions.

This thing fills me with pleasure. I don't know why, I can see it in the smallest detail. I find myself recalling it again and again, each time bringing more detail out of a sunken memory, remembering brings the curious warm pleasure.

It was very early in the morning. The eastern mountains were black-blue, but behind them the light stood up faintly colored at the mountain rims with a washed red, growing colder, greyer and darker as it went up and overhead until, at a place near the west, it merged with pure night.

And it was cold, not painfully so, but cold enough so that I rubbed my hands and shoved them deep into my pockets, and I hunched my shoulders up and scuffled my feet on the ground. Down in the valley where I was, the earth was that lavender grey of dawn. I walked along a country road and ahead of me I saw a tent that was only a little lighter grey than the ground. Beside the tent there was a flash of orange fire seeping out of the cracks of an old rusty iron stove. Grey smoke spurted up out of the stubby stovepipe, spurted up a long way before it spread out and dissipated.

I saw a young woman beside the stove, really a girl. She was dressed in a faded cotton skirt and waist. As I came close I saw that she carried a baby in a crooked arm and the baby was nursing, its head under her waist out of the cold. The mother moved about, poking the fire, shifting the rusty lids of the stove to make a greater draft, opening the oven door; and all the time the baby was nursing, but that didn't interfere with the mother's work, nor with the light quick gracefulness of her movements. There was something very precise and practiced in her movements. The orange fire flicked out of the cracks in the stove and threw dancing reflections on the tent.

I was close now and I could smell frying bacon and baking bread, the warmest, pleasantest odors I know. From the east the light grew swiftly. I came near to the stove and stretched my hands out to it and shivered all over when the warmth struck me. Then the tent flap jerked up and a young man came out and an older man followed him. They were dressed in new blue dungarees and in new dungaree coats with the brass buttons shining. They were sharp-faced men, and they looked much alike.

The younger had a dark stubble beard and the older had a grey stubble beard. Their heads and faces were wet, their hair dripped with water, and water stood out on their stiff beards and their cheeks shone with water. Together they stood looking quietly at the lightening east; they yawned together and looked at the light on the hill rims. They turned and saw me.

"Morning," said the older man. His face was neither friendly nor unfriendly.

"Morning, sir," I said.

"Morning," said the young man.

The water was slowly drying on their faces. They came to the stove and warmed their hands at it.

The girl kept to her work, her face averted and her eyes on what she was doing. Her hair was tied back out of her eyes with a string and it hung down her back and swayed as she worked. She set tin cups on a big packing box, set tin plates and knives and forks out too. Then she scooped fried bacon out of the deep grease and laid it on a big tin platter, and the bacon cricked and rustled as it grew crisp. She opened the rusty oven door and took out a square pan full of high big biscuits.

When the smell of that hot bread came out, both of the men inhaled deeply...

The elder man turned to me, "Had your breakfast?"

"No."

"Well sit down with us, then."

That was the signal. We went to the packing case and squatted on the ground about it. The young man asked, "Picking cotton?"

"No."

"We had twelve days' work so far," the young man said.

The girl spoke from the stove. "They even got new clothes."

The two men looked down at their new dungarees and they both smiled a little.

The girl set out the platter of bacon, the brown high

biscuits, a bowl of bacon gravy and a pot of coffee, and
then she squatted down by the box too. The baby was
still nursing, its head up under her waist out of the cold.
I could hear the suckling noises it made.

We filled our plates, poured bacon gravy over our
biscuits and sugared our coffee. The older man filled his
mouth full and he chewed and chewed and
swallowed...

The young man said, "We been eating good for twelve
days."

We all ate quickly, frantically, and refilled our plates
and ate quickly again until we were full and warm. The
hot bitter coffee scalded our throats. We threw the last bit
with the grounds in it on the earth and refilled our cups.

There was color in the light now, a reddish gleam that
made the air seem colder. The two men faced the east
and their faces were lighted by the dawn, and I looked
up for a moment and saw the image of the mountain
and the light coming over it reflected in the older man's
eyes.

Then the two men threw the grounds from their cups on
the earth and they stood up together. "Got to get going,"
the older man said.

The younger turned to me. "F' you want to pick cotton,
we could maybe get you on."

"No. I got to go along. Thanks for breakfast."

The older man waved his hand in a negative. "O.K.
Glad to have you." They walked away together. The air
was blazing with light at the eastern skyline. And I

walked away down the country road.

That's all. I know, of course, some of the reasons why it was pleasant. But there was some element of great beauty there that makes the rush of warmth when I think of it.

Here is a list of specific questions to ask yourself about Steinbeck's narrative. Write your answers to these questions in your notebook.

1. What did they have to eat? How does Steinbeck make it sound so delicious?
2. What colors do you remember from this description? What smells? What visual images?
3. Do you think that you would like these people? Why?
4. Steinbeck says, "I know, of course, some of the reasons why it was pleasant." What <u>are</u> some of these reasons?
5. Do have any warm memories about special meals you have eaten?
6. Have you ever met anyone just once who has made a lasting impression on you? What was this person like?

Next, read the narrative below, "Subject Matter for a Daydream" by Karl Swinehart, a student. In this narrative, he presents an experience he had while on a trip in the upper reaches of Lake Huron. Notice especially the sensory descriptions that Karl uses.

Subject Matter for a Daydream

"It's beautiful," were my sister's awe-inspired words as we watched the sun setting over the earth's edge. We were in the upper reaches of Lake Huron, in a group of islands that make up the North Channel. These islands are like none other; they are made of rose granite (what those pink stone baths are made from). They rise out of the water like the backs of huge pink whales.

We trudged back down to where the water met rock, hopped in the little dinghy, and rowed to the boat to sleep...The rocking motion, back and forth, swept me into a fetal sleep.

Sunshine on the ceiling and a foul taste in my mouth brought me into the new day. I got up and put bowls around for breakfast, as someone else was doing something equally if not more helpful. Granola was our morning staple; I felt like we belonged in a Grape Nuts commercial. As my sisters and I were eating breakfast, a big boney white Bandolf pulled its wet, half naked body onto the boat. It was Wickham, my dad's Australian cohort and the more or less unofficial captain of the boat, the Yo-Yo.

"The water is superb—you should be woken yup by it," he said, as cheery as a puppy, referring to the 57 degree water, as he dried himself briskly with a green towel.

So, being young and impressionable I took his advice, only vaguely knowing how extreme the temperature actually was. I, as eager as a chimpanzee (however eager they may be), put on my swimtrunks. Prancing

*out to the edge of the boat, the air on my bare skin
cracked the ignorance about how cold it truly was that
morning in the Northern Channel. I stared down
beyond my toes, which were clinched tightly around the
boat's edge, into the deep, clear greenness. Why was it so
clear? Was it because it was too intensely cold for plant
life to grow?*

*Jumping into the icy blue water, I knew I was right
about the plants. My heart stopped and started with
hesitancy. As I sunk into the deepness, the coldness
seemed to try to pull me down as I bobbed back up
toward the surface. My eyeballs screamed at me for
subjecting them to such low temperatures. My muscles
were constricted in shock. Never before had they felt
anything colder. Mr. Body finally adjusted, and I could
swim. Let it be known, however, that it was a mighty
brief swim, but I did do it. The waters of the North
Channel were conquered, and I had done it. After my
initial meeting with the water, I had many other
rendezvous.*

*We don't sail through the North Channel anymore. The
Yo-Yo hasn't seen our groggy faces on brisk, sunny
mornings. But, on rainy days indoors, or on a blustery
winter morning I can believe in the blue waters of the
North Channel.*

Karl Swinehart

Here are some questions about Karl's narrative and
about your own experiences outdoors. Write the
answers to these questions in your notebook.

1. Does this experience sound like something you
would want to try yourself? Why or why not?

2. If jumping into the water was such an uncomfortable thing to do, why do you suppose the writer did it so many times?

3. How does the writer get across the feelings of intense cold that he experiences?

4. When were you the coldest you have ever been? The hottest? The muddiest? The craziest?

5. Have you ever done something physically difficult just to see if you could do it? What did you do?

Before you begin to write your significant experience narrative, it might help to read several remarks from professional writers about how they draw material from their own lives. Writers first and foremost write about themselves—their experiences, feelings, hopes, and dreams. And that's where you will need to start, too. On a separate sheet of paper, write down the quote you find most interesting.

The truth is, I have never written a story in my life that didn't have a very firm foundation in actual human experience—somebody else's experience quite often....
—Katherine Anne Porter

As a writer I think background matters most in how well it teaches you to look around and see clearly what's there and in how deeply it nourishes your imagination.
—Eudora Welty

If a writer stops observing he is finished. But he does not have to observe consciously nor think how it will be useful.
—Ernest Hemingway

I don't really care whether I find a form that enchants others as much as I care about finding something that can delight me from day to day as I work it out.
—*Gore Vidal*

The greatness of a writer has nothing to do with subject matter itself, only with how much the subject matter touches the author.
—*Boris Pasternak*

Brainstorming

Now you need to focus upon a significant event in your life. As a warm-up, take a few minutes to write in your journal. Try the topic, "Hollywood is making a movie of my life—what scenes should it include?"

Below are some probing questions to get you started.

People

• Who are the most important people in your life? Why are they so important to you?
• If you were kidnapped by aliens from another planet, who would you miss the most? Why?
• Have you ever had a close friend move away? How did that make you feel? Have you ever seen him or her again? Did things seem the same or were they different?
• How did you meet your best friend? How did you become so close?

Places

• Imagine that you and your family were going to go

to live in a space colony, never to return to earth again. Where would you visit before you left?

• Where would you never want to go again? Why not?

• Where did the happiest moment of your life take place? The saddest? The scariest? The funniest? The strangest?

Growing Up

• What were some of the hardest decisions you ever had to make? Looking back now, do you think you made the right decisions?

• If you could go back in time to one moment in your life, which would it be? Why would you pick that moment? Would you do anything different this time than you did then?

• How are you a different person now than you were the day you entered first grade? What has happened to make you different?

Step Two: Composing

Creating a Draft of a Narrative

Write a draft of your narrative. The length of your narrative will vary, depending upon the experience you choose to describe, but a good length to aim for is two to three pages. Short narratives tend to lack details, and longer narratives tend to ramble on because they are unfocused.

You can write about any significant experience. Someone writing about a single experience will probably want to organize it chronologically—that is, what happened first, second, third, and so forth. If you write about a series of related experiences, organize your narrative by ideas. For example, you might choose to write about a series of times one summer when you went swimming with some friends in a river. For this kind of narrative, you will want to explore the ideas behind the events: 1) how you all decided to go swimming, 2) why you chose to go to the river, 3) how the events there affected you and your friends, and so forth.

The key at this first stage is to get your entire narrative down on paper. Correct grammar, punctuation, and sentence mechanics need not be perfect the first time around. You will have an opportunity to edit and proofread later. For now, the goal is a workable draft of your narrative.

Step Three: Revising

The next few pages provide a number of activities to enable you to improve the drafts of your narrative. The first activity will help you understand that writing is (and should be) influenced by the writer's awareness of a particular audience for which the writing is intended. The second activity shows you how to select the "right words"—the specific and vivid words that make descriptions interesting. The third provides you with practice in combining sentences. The peer response sheet involves you in editing the endings of narratives and in selecting vivid words for papers.

Understanding Your Audience

When doing any writing, you need to understand who your audience is. Most young writers think that teachers are their only audience. But, when you do creative writing, other students and adults may often be your audience as well.

An experienced writer can write a good narrative because he or she understands how to adapt writing for different audiences. You, too, should develop this ability to change your writing style depending upon your material, purpose, and audience. The following activity will show you how.

Imagine that you are involved in the following situation:

You are sitting in your school's cafeteria eating lunch. Your worst enemy comes over carrying a tray with a large piece of cherry pie and a carton of milk on it. Your enemy sits down across the table from you and accuses you of having stolen some pencils. You have not, of course, stolen the pencils, so you ignore your enemy. This makes your enemy very angry. Your enemy starts yelling at you, so you shout back, telling your enemy to get lost. The cafeteria supervisor, a large and grumpy physical education teacher, hears the shouting and comes over toward your table. Just as the physical education teacher arrives at the table, your enemy picks up the piece of cherry pie and hurls it at you. You duck, and the pie hits the physical education teacher right in the stomach. The teacher's new white shirt and face are the exact same color red. This seems hilarious to most of the students, but you and your enemy are hauled off to the principal's office.

You have not done anything wrong. But the principal, who doesn't know this, asks you to explain, in writing, exactly what happened. You are a little bit afraid of the principal. You want to make sure that your explanation doesn't get you into more trouble. The best course seems to be brief and state the facts. In your notebook, write your explanation to the principal.

When you return to your class you learn that your language arts teacher has heard about "The Great Cafeteria Cherry Pie Incident." He also asks you to explain what happened in writing. You like your teacher, and you know your teacher likes you. You are inclined with him to make the story amusing. Write your explanation to your teacher.

Now you have to tell your friends. Write a note to your best friend who was not in the cafeteria when the incident occurred. Explain what happened, how you feel about the incident, and what you think of the other student.

Look at your three explanations. Notice how your use of words changed for each audience. What parts of the incident did you emphasize in each note? What parts did you change as your audience changed?

Editing Activity

Choosing the Right Word

Choosing the right word will enable you to make your writing more interesting. Specific words create a clearer picture in writing than general words do. *House* and *shack*, for example, are more specific than *building*. *Stroll* and *stomp* are more specific than *walk*. Chat and *argue* are more specific than *talk*.

To see how writers select words and to learn how to choose the best words for your writing, complete this activity:

A. Compare this sentence to the brief paragraph about a butterfly.

—A butterfly by the window flies into the building.

—A butterfly, wings shivering, clings to the metal grating over the shack window. Drawn perhaps to light, perhaps to warmth, it dips and swings into the shack, hovering in the rafters.

Notice that the writer of the paragraph has included sensory imagery to show the butterfly's actions. Notice also that the writer has chosen specific words to show the butterfly's movements. It clings, dips, swings, and hovers. Specific words like these verbs make the picture the writer creates in the reader's mind more clear and vivid. Notice, when you read, how good writers tend to use strong—and quite specific—verbs.

B. Now read this passage about a rainstorm at a harbor. Each of the missing verbs means "to move." Write a specific, vivid action verb in each of the blanks.

The storm, blowing for a third day, **1.)** _____ ten-foot waves onto the seawall at the mouth of the harbor. Most of the waves break onto the wall, **2.)** _____ spray into the channel. A few, however, **3.)** _____ over the embankment, breaking full force as they descend. Even the multi-ton barge **4.)** _____ against the wooden pilings in the outer channel. Sailboat masts **5.)** _____ from side to side; cruisers **6.)** _____ on their moorings. The wind **7.)** _____ at the boats, **8.)** _____ them loose from the blocks and chains that link them to the harbor floor.

C. Compare your word choices to the words the writer originally used:

1. pulls	**2.** hurtling	**3.** roll	**4.** clangs
5. swing	**6.** rock	**7.** yanks	**8.** tearing

In your notebook, tell how your words are similar to the writer's and how they are different.

Notice that the words are simple and direct, not long and fancy. They describe what the wind and rain are doing to the water and boats. The right words are often like these examples: brief, straightforward, and vivid.

Vivid Language by Professional Writers

To become adept at choosing the right word, you need to learn how to read like a writer. Most writers watch the way other writers phrase things. They examine how words are used in every sentence they read. What twist has the writer put on the words? What words were new to you? Which sound especially good?

Read the passage below from *Great Expectations* by Charles Dickens.

A fearful man, all in coarse grey, with a great iron on his leg. A man with no hat, and with broken shoes, and with an old rag tied round his head. A man who had been soaked in water, and smothered in mud, and lamed by stones, and cut by flints, and stung by nettles, and torn by briars; who limped, and shivered, and glared, and growled; and whose teeth chattered in his head, as he seized me by the chin.

1. Which words do you find the most vivid?

_____

_____

2. How would you react to seeing this man? Why?

_____

_____

_____

_____

Here are some other examples of good narratives that you might want to look up.

1. Toni Cade Bambara's "Raymond's Run" (the run itself)
2. Jack London's *The Call of the Wild,* Chapter Four (the fight between Buck and Spitz)
3. Irwin Shaw's "The 80 Yard Run," Paragraph 1 (the run itself)
4. John Steinbeck's "Flight," Paragraph 1 (description of the Torres farm)
5. Mark Twain's *The Adventures of Huckleberry Finn,* Chapters Six and Sixteen (Pap attacks Huck; the steamboat crash)

Now, apply this idea of using specific and direct words to your editing of your own writing. In your notebook, rewrite your description of the most important moment, the critical event in your narrative.

Then, expand that description. Use sensory details and specific descriptive words to really show that moment to your readers. Choose each word so that it gives the exact meaning you want.

Sentence Combining

One excellent way to improve your writing is to combine short, choppy sentences into longer, smoother ones. By combining sentences, you are able to say what you want in fewer words. Here is an example:

—The school was large. It was made of red bricks. I was a little scared. I entered the front door.

These four sentences can be combined like this:

—I was a little scared as I entered the front door of the large, red-brick school.

Notice that all the information of the four sentences is present in the one combined sentence. The four sentences use twenty words to make the point. The combined sentence, which no longer sounds choppy, uses only sixteen.

Here are ten sets of sentences taken from narratives written by beginning writers. Combine each of these sets of sentences into one sentence. Then, read over each sentence you have created to make sure that it sounds good to you. Compare each of your combined sentences with those you started with. Often there is more than one good way to combine sentences.

1. It was December 17th. We all gathered at my house.

_____

_____

_____

2. The bowling alley we were going to was Classic Bowl. It is located on Waukegan Road.

_____

_____

_____

3. After the long bus ride, Preston and I ran to our houses. Preston is a close neighbor and a good friend.

_____

_____

_____

4. It was a gloomy and chilly Christmas Eve. My family and I went to my aunt's house to celebrate.

_____

_____

_____

5. My fortress was a super multi-function facility. The fortress consisted of four rooms to aid in battle.

_____

_____

_____

6. It was first grade. I was playing on the playground. I was swinging on the swing.

_____

_____

_____

7. It was around the time when I was a little boy. I think I was about five to seven years of age. It was the day after Christmas. All of the family had gifts to use.

_____

_____

_____

8. In the clearing was a fence. It was quite an interesting fence. Each twig in it was about two feet long.

_____

_____

_____

9. The witch had no broom to fly on. She always stayed in one place. This was her hideaway.

_____

_____

_____

10. I was seven years old. The monster lived in the house. Every night when I went to bed, I had to confront it.

_____

_____

_____

Now reread your narrative. Find two or three sentences that you think can be combined. Combine those sentences into one longer, smoother sentence.

Count the words in your original sentences and the words in your combined sentence. How many words have you saved by combining the sentences?

Combine other choppy sentences in your narrative. For additional sentence combining activities, see pages 134–136 in the *Writer's Supplement* in the back of this handbook.

Transitions

Here is another list of words and phrases to use as transitions. Transitions can help summarize, introduce conflicting ideas or events, and present cause-and-effect relationships:

all in all	conversely
as a matter of fact	frankly
as it happens	likewise
at any rate	needless to say
better yet	nonetheless
by chance	on the contrary
consequently	otherwise
whereas	

Peer Editing

At this point you should let your peer editor respond to your significant event narrative. Have the editor focus especially on your word choices and on your ending and your word choices.

1. Complete this statement: Things I liked best were...
2. Finish this sentence: Things I would like to know more about were...
3. How has the writer wrapped up the narrative? What do you like or dislike about this ending?
4. Suggest a different way to end the narrative.
5. Improve three word choices by substituting more vivid language. For example: walk (writer's word), strut (better word).
6. Suggest which short, choppy sentences can be combined into longer, smoother sentences.

Writing the Final Draft

Read through your narrative carefully, making any changes you think will improve your writing. Think about your peer editor's comments. Expand sensory descriptions, especially of the most important moments in the narrative. Choose the right words for every scene. Combine sentences and add transitions. Then, write out a final, public copy of your narrative that can be shared with other people.

Proofreading

Before finishing the final copy of your narrative, reread it aloud one more time to correct errors. Remember that in the *Writer's Supplement* at the end of this handbook, there is a review of English style and usage. Use this information to enable you to proofread your narrative with confidence.

Unit 4: Creating a Short Story

Writing short fiction can sometimes be more difficult than writing narratives. In traditional short stories, you need to understand the points of view and story structure. Through short stories, you can come to understand better the fundamental elements of short fiction—what it takes to create a character, how to manage a plot, and so on. This new understanding will soon transfer over to your own reading of fiction. In other words, by becoming a better writer you will become a better reader as well.

In this unit you will learn to:

- Understand the structural elements of the short story.
- Understand the various points of view used in the narration of the short story.
- Use dialogue effectively in writing.
- Compose a traditional short story with plot, setting, and characters.
- Develop guidelines for the evaluation of short stories.
- Edit short stories in terms of structure and style.

Step One: Prewriting

Because we do not usually write fiction the way we write narratives, let's begin with several prewriting activities which focus on:

- point of view in a story
- structure of short fiction
- characterization
- use of dialogue in writing.

You will also read an example of student writing and have a chance to do some brainstorming before you begin your own story.

Point of View

To understand better the various points of view from which a story can be told, complete the following activity. This activity also serves as an excellent bridge from first-person narrative writing to third-person fiction writing.

1st person—main character

The central character in the story is telling the story. This narrator uses "I" and tells the reader his or her thoughts.

1st person—observer

A less important character in the story is telling the story about the main character. This narrator uses "I" and tells the reader his or her thoughts but not the main character's thoughts.

3rd person—all-knowing (omniscient)

A voice outside the story is telling the story. This narrator does not use "I" but rather "he" or "she" to describe the characters and action in the story. This narrator also informs the readers what the characters are thinking.

3rd person—reporter (bird's eye view)

A voice outside the story is telling the story. This narrator does not use "I" but rather "he" or "she" to describe the characters and action in the story. This narrator, however, does not inform the readers what the characters are thinking.

A. Imagine a scene. Enter Mr. Smythe, Killer, and Spike.

Imagine you are seated in the mathematics classroom. Mr. Smythe is lecturing for the fifteenth consecutive day on the finer aspects of the decimal point. Most of the students are dozing, but a boy (Killer) and a girl (Spike) in the back of the room are whispering to each other. Because he is so involved in the wonders of the decimal point, Mr. Smythe ignores them until Killer passes a note to Spike.

This sort of disrespect (not only for his teaching but also for the decimal point) causes Mr. Smythe to go crazy. He throws his hands into the air, rushes to the back of the room, and takes the note from a bewildered Spike. Suddenly, Killer tries to grab the note from Mr. Smythe. A huge struggle occurs, and eventually Mr. Symthe obtains the note. Waving it and laughing, he runs triumphantly to the front of the classroom.

In your notebook, write this scene using one of the 3rd-person points of view that follow:

• 3rd-person all-knowing—includes Mr. Smythe's, Spike's, and Killer's thoughts.
• 3rd-person reporter—describes the events that occurred in vivid detail.

B. Now, imagine how the story changes as the point of view changes. What changes in language and descriptions would occur if Killer were telling the story? What parts of the story would he emphasize?

C. What changes in language and descriptions would occur if Mr. Smythe were telling the story? What parts of the story would he emphasize?

Short Story Structure

Unlike the personal narrative, which is based on an actual incident or incidents in a writer's life, the short story is based on imaginary characters and events. Good writers, of course, draw upon their own experiences and observations to create characters and situations that are believable and interesting.

Since the possibilities for devising characters and situations is infinite, short stories can be created in countless ways. However, no matter if the story is realistic or bizarre, local or exotic, horrifying or heartwarming, all short stories possess a **plot**, or a series of actions containing certain key **elements**.

You have probably experienced the confusing feeling of turning on a television or walking into a movie theater after a film has long since started. It is difficult to catch up with what is going on. Who are these people? Where are they? When is this taking place? What has already happened? The reason it all seems so baffling is that you have missed the **exposition**, or important introductory information. Without that, it is hard to understand, or even to care about, what is happening to these people.

As we learn the important information of the exposition, we soon determine who is the central character or **protagonist**. This is the person or persons whose actions and decisions we follow throughout the plot. It is not enough merely to have a protagonist— this character must also be faced with some sort of problem or obstacle with which he or she must deal. This can be as ordinary as a decision to cheat or not on a science test or as extraordinary as a battle to the death with a killer shark. Either way, this problem, or **conflict**, is the key to any traditional short story.

As the story progresses, the problem that the protagonist faces will become more complicated. This **complication**, or **rising action**, will often consist of a number of incidents, or **crises**. These lead the protagonist towards the important scene in which the problem is finally settled one way or the other—called the **climax**. All that remains at this point is the aftermath, or **denouement**, which wraps up any remaining loose ends.

The chart on the next page should help you picture how these central elements tie together to produce a complete plot. To remind yourself of how this works, recall the storyline of a well-known short story, "The Three Little Pigs." Notice how this information fits neatly into the structure of the basic short story.

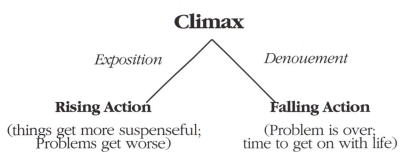

Climax

Exposition *Denouement*

Rising Action

(things get more suspenseful;
Problems get worse)

Falling Action

(Problem is over;
time to get on with life)

Crisis	**Crisis**	**Crisis**
Wolf destroys straw house; eats Pig #1	*Wolf destroys twig house; eats Pig # 2*	*Wolf is frustrated by initial attempts on brick house*

Climax

Wolf tries chimney trick, but is outwitted by Pig # 3 and gets boiled!

Denouement

Pig # 3 cleans up mess; feels smug about brick purchase

Below is a diagram of the classic structure of a traditional short story that will enable you to work out the plot of your own story:

Climax

Exposition *Denouement*

Rising Action

(Things get more suspenseful;
problems get worse.)

Falling Action

(Problem is over;
time to get on with life.)

Crisis   **Crisis**   **Crisis**

Characterization

There are essentially two methods that a writer can use in order to describe a character. First, a writer can come right out and state what he wants to say through **direct characterization.** For example, the writer states:

—Killer was a really mean guy. Everyone hated him.

An advantage of this method is that the writer is sure to get the necessary information across to the reader.

But in real life, we form our own opinions about people much differently. We notice what they do. We listen to what they say. We hear what other people say about them. Then we draw our own conclusions. An author can let us learn about the characters in much the same way through **indirect characterization**. Notice how much more effective this passage is when we observe this information—that is, when we are shown as opposed to being told.

—Killer barged into the cafeteria and grabbed the smallest kid there by his shirt collar. "Get lost, pee wee!" he hollered. "This is my seat now." Suzanne turned to Debbie and whispered, "He thinks he's so cool, but I think he's just a big jerk!" "So do I!" agreed Debbie.

Notice that one of the most effective ways to liven up a short story is by including dialogue between the characters. Listen to your television any night of the week, and you will discover that creating realistic dialogue is a challenge even to professional writers. Somehow people in stories don't always seem to talk like people in real life. Part of this can be explained by the fact that authors often rely on dialogue to serve as a method of providing expository information. ("Hello, I'm just back from seven years in the African Congo. Now what's this I hear about you folks being involved in a particularly thrilling murder mystery?") But more often it stems from something else.

When writing dialogue, it is useful to ask yourself two key questions: 1) Is there some reason for including this piece of conversation? and 2) Do people really talk this way?

The answer to the first question is usually easy enough. Just ask yourself if the passage gives the reader a clearer understanding of the characters. If not, then does it advance the action of the plot? To answer the second question, though, a writer must learn to develop a good ear for dialogue. Generally, that requires years of practice. From now on listen to what people say in everyday conversation—listen to which words are used and to how people pronounce words.

The key to writing effective dialogue is to make it *sound* like everyday speech but *be* more coherent, without the hemming and hawing and sputtering. To learn—and use—the natural patterns of spoken English in written dialogue, complete the following activity. This activity also provides you with the opportunity to work on plot structure.

1. "Collect" a conversation in your notebook. Eavesdrop on and write down a conversation in the school cafeteria, the playground, the neighborhood, a local store, or at home. Record as well as possible whatever was said word-for-word. You can, of course, inform the people that you are jotting down the dialogue, but this tends to have the same effect on people that handing them a microphone does; it often destroys "natural" speech rhythms.

2. Now read your transcript aloud. These literal transcripts almost always sound like jibberish for two reasons. First, the context of the conversation is missing. Also, people often talk in circles. Entirely real conversation—obviously—won't work in short stories. You have to improve on it while remembering dialogue in fiction should *sound* like it is real speech.

3. Use a few lines of the dialogue that you collected as the basis for a short story scene. That is, mix the setting, the descriptions of the persons, the actions, and the dialogue you collected into a brief "fictional excerpt." Share your excerpt with other people to discover if it sounds to them like real dialogue.

Exploring Ideas

"Fire!," a short story by a young writer named Brad Mitchell, appears below. As you read it, pay particular attention to the details about firefighting and the way dialogue is used. Note how Brad works the information he has learned about firefighting into this story.

FIRE!

"Oh, thank God you're home. It's nine o'clock, Jack. I've been worried about you," she said, as Jack entered the kitchen. "I saved some dinner for you. It's in the refrigerator. You can heat it up in the microwave."

"Thanks," Jack replied, as he hung up his red firefighter's hat, covered with soot, on the hook on the

wall. His dark brown hair was matted with sweat, and his blue eyes looked weary. His big, but gentle, hands were also covered in soot and ash.

"We had a big grassfire over in one of the vacant lots by the high school. It wouldn't have been so bad if one of the pumpers wasn't on an ambulance run when the fire was called in."

"Don't you ever get frightened, Jack? I'm scared to death that one day you'll be brought back from a fire as just a pile of ashes," she said. "Why don't you stick with your real job? You've got a family to think about."

Jack turned from the microwave to look at his wife. "Not this again," he thought. "Ann, you know I love fighting fires," he replied.

"But you're a good accountant. Why can't you just work with numbers? They're a lot safer than fires. You don't even get paid for risking your life at the fires," Anne said, concerned.

Jack sat down at the table with his reheated dinner and began to eat. He didn't really know why he loved being a volunteer fireman. It wasn't really the danger. Ann was right. He did have a wife and kids to look after, and he was working his way up the corporate ladder. "I don't know, OK? I just don't know!" After toying with his food for a few, silent seconds, Jack looked up again.

"How did Mike do in his soccer game today?" asked Jack, changing the subject.

"His team won, but he cut his shin near the end and stayed out the rest of the game," Ann responded.

Jack finished his late dinner and carried his plate to the sink. He rinsed it off and then placed it in the dishwasher. He started up the stairs, wrapping his arm around his wife. She looked up at him and smiled faintly.

After looking into his kids' bedrooms and kissing each of his sleeping children, he made his way to his own bedroom, undressed and slipped into the comfortable bed. The fire fighting had exhausted him; he fell asleep almost immediately.

******

"We have a structure on fire at the corner of Oak Street and Lion Court. Please respond."

The silence was broken as the message boomed over the fire radio. Jack rubbed his eyes as he sat up in bed. Gazing at the clock, he blinked a few times, trying to wake himself. He started to dress in the dark, quickly pulling on his jeans.

"What time is it?" asked Ann, rolling over in bed and opening her big, brown eyes a slight bit.

"Two thirty," replied Jack, as he slipped a T-shirt over his head.

"Go back to sleep, Jack," said Ann. "You have to go to work tomorrow."

Jack looked at his wife as she buried her head in the pillow. As Jack hurried down the hall, his daughter peered sleepily out of her room. "Where are you going, Daddy?" she mumbled sleepily.

"I have to go to a fire. Go back to sleep, Kelly."

Jack raced down the stairs and grabbed his fire jacket and hat on the way out the door. He was almost out the door when he turned back. Picking his keys up off the old washing machine, he exited the house for the second time. After fumbling with the keys in the dark for a few seconds, Jack opened the car door and jumped in. He plugged his rotating light into the cigarette lighter and fastened it to the roof as he pulled out of the driveway. In his haste, he didn't notice his wife staring out the second story window at him.

On his way to the fire, Jack picked up the mouthpiece of the two way radio. "713 responding to the fire," he said, and returned the mouthpiece to the radio.

"Oh no," he said to himself, as he rounded the corner and the building came into view. A four story apartment building was ablaze, sending smoke high up into the atmosphere. Flames burst out through the windows and jumped up the building wall. Evacuated tenants stood all over the area, staring at the burning structure.

Two of the fire engines had already arrived, and a handful of firefighters were rigging up the hoses. Jack parked his car a good one hundred and fifty feet from the building, but the heat was still intense. He immediately radioed in for mutual aid, and surrounding fire departments started responding.

As Jack flipped his visor down and started towards the fire, a lady rushed towards him, screaming hysterically. "Calm down," he said.

"My baby! My baby is inside! Save him, please! My baby!"

Jack's eyes doubled in size. He thought about Kelly, greeting him at the door after a hard day at work, and Mike playing in his soccer game. Pushing the lady aside, he called for the aluminum suit. The boots of the other firemen started to smoke from the intense heat, and other men hosed them down to prevent heat exhaustion. As Jack slipped into the cumbersome suit, he asked the woman what room the child was in. Through her sobs, she replied, "208."

Slipping his air tank onto his back, Jack plunged into the flaming building. The building was turning into a fire storm, sending ashes and live embers rocketing through the air. A huge explosion warned Jack not to enter. He pushed through the burning rubble and climbed the stairs.

Jack entered the hallway of the second story. This particular wing had not suffered much damage, but the smoke alone was enough to kill a person. Jack only had a few minutes of air himself before the tank would run out. The doors being too charred to read numbers, Jack kicked the first door in—nothing. The second door fell with a thud and the same result was reached—nothing. He continued to knock down doors and search rooms, as his tank continued to empty.

Jack kicked another door down, and this time he heard someone crying. He ran towards the sound and found a young boy, about four years old Jack guessed, huddled on the floor, crying. Jack wrapped up the boy in the bedspread to protect him from the heat of the suit, and started out the door. Part of the ceiling in the hall collapsed into flames.

The air from the tank expired just as Jack escaped the burning building. The boy was lowered into one of the ambulances waiting outside. Jack stripped his suit off, and a wave of heat hit him. Some of the surrounding houses had caught fire, but most of the raging fire was under control.

Jack trudged further away from the fire, and then he collapsed on the ground—his energy spent. He got up after a few minutes and treaded towards his car. The plastic light on top of his car had melted, and opening the car door was a painful ordeal. "I'll just go home and take a cold shower," he thought, looking at his black hands. He started away, struggling to stay awake.

Jack entered his house as the sun rose up in the east. Stripping to his jeans, he lay down on the couch, falling asleep almost instantly.

Hearing the door open, Ann softly descended the stairs. She entered the family room, to find her husband asleep on the couch. She stared at his filthy hands and face and thought about sending him upstairs to clean up. Then she shook her head in disbelief and smiled. She walked up the stairs and went back to sleep.

******

Jack parked the car in the garage and walked to the back door. He held his briefcase in one hand and pulled his tie loose with the other. He knocked on the door and listened as tiny feet scuttled to the door. Kelly opened the door and let him in.

"How was work, honey?" Ann asked him from the kitchen.

*"Oh, all right I suppose. We just got another big client,"
Jack replied.*

*"The chief stopped by today with this. He said to give it to
you." Ann handed Jack a small white envelope. "I still
don't understand why you like fighting fires so much."*

*Jack ripped open the envelope, wondering what it
contained. He pulled the letter out and unfolded it. A
picture of a four year old fell to the table. He read the
letter and then, with shaking hands, placed the picture
of the boy in his wallet, right behind the pictures of his
own children.*

*Then Jack softly replied to his wife, "It's the rewards,"
and Jack pocketed his wallet.*

Brad Mitchell

Here is a list of specific questions to ask yourself about
the story. Write the answers in your notebook.

1. What did you learn about firefighting from reading
this story that you hadn't known before?
2. How does the writer help us to get a sense of what
fighting a fire is like?
3. What do you think is the most interesting scene in
this story? What details has the writer used to make it
seem exciting?
4. How does Jack's wife feel about Jack being a
firefighter? Why do you think she feels that way?
5. Do you think Jack will continue to be a firefighter?
Why or why not?

Brainstorming

Short story ideas come from a variety of sources. An idea may come from something that has happened to you; it may come from a story told to you by a friend or someone in your family; or an idea may come to you from something you read in the paper or hear on television. No one source is the best. Writers simply keep themselves open to ideas.

Below are some questions you can ask yourself to help generate ideas for stories.

The Writer

• When were you most nervous? Most excited? Most afraid? Most angry?
• What special interests do you have? What subjects do you know about that others do not?
• Have you ever been involved in an accident or otherwise injured?

Family and Friends

• What is the best thing that ever happened to someone you know? The worst thing?
• What special interests or skills does someone you know have?
• What important events have occurred in your family's past? How did your relatives get to America? How did your parents and grandparents meet?

The World

- What conflicts occur in your neighborhood?
- What issues have recently been in the news?
- What news stories do you remember that especially interested you?
- What books, movies, and TV shows have been especially memorable?
- Which of your answers to these questions could be used as a starting point or a climax of a story?

Finally, if you have trouble coming up with short story ideas, you should remind yourself that you have *already* created the material for short stories. Choose one of your narratives created in one of the earlier chapters. Turn it into a short story with a third-person narrator and a traditional plot.

Professional Writers on Writing Short Fiction

Here are some comments by professional writers about writing short stories. They may help you understand better how other writers feel about writing short stories. In your notebook, copy any quotation that you find interesting or helpful.

I know I was writing stories when I was five. I don't remember what I did before that. Just loafed, I suppose.... I can't think of myself as anything but a writer.
—P.G. Wodehouse

To my mind, a fiction writer's honesty begins right there,

*in being true to those two facts of time and place. From
there, imagination can take him anywhere.*
—Eudora Welty

*Mostly you invent people from a knowledge and
understanding and experience of people.*
—Ernest Hemingway

You can't write about people out of textbooks.
—Katherine Anne Porter

*To write fiction, one needs a whole series of inspirations
about people in an actual environment, and then a
whole lot of hard work on the basis of those inspirations.*
—Isaac Bashevis Singer

Fiction is meant to illuminate, to explode, to refresh.
—John Cheever

*The language must be careful and must appear
effortless. It must not sweat. It must suggest and be
provocative at the same time.*
—Toni Morrison

*If you are using dialogue—say it aloud as you write it.
Only then will it have the sound of speech.*
—John Steinbeck

*Dialogue… has so many ways to function. Sometimes I
needed to make a speech do three or four or five things
at once—reveal what the character said but also what
he thought he said, what he hid, what others were going
to think he meant, what they misunderstood, and so
forth—all in his single speech.*
—Eudora Welty

Step Two: Composing

Creating a Draft of a Short Story

Using the most promising idea you thought about while brainstorming, write a draft of a short story. The length of the story you draft will vary from that of other writers, depending upon your age, skill, and the sophistication of your writing. That is to be expected. Besides, length is never an indicator of how good a story is. Make your story as long or as short as it needs to be, but a good average length to aim for is two to four pages. Stories that are too short tend to lack plot development and sensory details.

The key at this stage is to get the entire short story down in your notebook. Correct grammar, punctuation, and mechanics matter, of course, but there will be an opportunity later to edit and proofread the draft. For now, your goal is a workable draft.

Step Three: Revising

Begin the process of revision by examining the structure of your story. The following peer response activity can help you analyze and respond to a story's plot. You may want to involve a friend as a peer editor at this stage. Then you or your friend can use the peer response activity below to evaluate the development of characters in the story. Finally, if you involve someone else in this editing stage, he or she can help you develop guidelines for analyzing short fiction.

Peer Response Activity

Exposition

1. When/Where does this story take place?
2. What has happened before?

Conflict and Climax

3. What problems does the central character face?
4. When do you learn how the problem is worked out?

Denouement

5. How does the story end?
6. Suggest an extra scene to strengthen the plot.

Peer Response Activity

Characterization

1. Who are the characters involved in the story? How would you describe their roles?
2. Direct Characterization: What does the author tell us "directly" about the protagonist (main character) from his or her physical appearance and personality?
3. Indirect Characterization: What do we learn "indirectly" about the protagonist from what he or she

says (does)? What do we learn about the protagonist from what others say about him or her?

4. Suggest an added detail to strengthen the description of one major or minor character.

Short Story Editing

Write for two or three minutes in your notebook on the following question: "If you were trying to help a friend improve his or her story, what elements of the story would you try to examine?" Make a list of the elements that come to mind.

For example, if you decide that "openings" are important, you might ask, "Does this opening catch the reader's attention?" If you select "dialogue" as an area to improve, you might ask, "Does the dialogue seem natural or phony?"

Either alone or with a friend, make a list in your notebook of ten questions that you would use to edit a short story draft.

Writing the Final Draft

Read through the draft of your short story, making any changes you think will improve your writing. Think about your peer editor's comments about the story's structure and characterizations. Make sure that the dialogue sounds like real speech. Expand sensory description and choose the right words for every scene.

Check your story in relation to all ten editing questions you wrote. Combine sentences and add transitions wherever necessary. Then, write out a final, public copy of your narrative that can be shared with other people.

Proofreading

After you have made all of the revisions that you think your story needs and then written a final draft of it, go back over your story to correct any mechanical errors. Remember that the *Writer's Supplement* at the end of this handbook includes information about both style and usage. Use this information to enable you to proofread your story with confidence.

Unit 5: Writing Poetry

For many people, the idea of writing poetry is baffling or even frightening, but writing poetry is in many ways just like writing anything else. The process involves gathering thoughts and images (prewriting), writing a draft of the poem (composing), and improving the poem (editing and proofreading). In fact, everything that we have stressed earlier in this handbook about good writing applies also to poetry. Poetry can, therefore, serve as a review of all of creative writing. Once you learn the structural and stylistic elements of poetry, you can transfer that understanding of and care for language to all of your writing. In other words, by becoming a better poet you will become a better writer.

In this unit, you will learn to:

- Understand the structural elements of poetry.
- Understand and use sensory imagery in poetry.
- Understand and use figurative language in poetry.
- Understand and use rhythms in poetry.
- Compose lyric poems.
- Develop guidelines for the evaluation of poems.
- Edit poems in terms of structure, style, and meaning.

In this chapter you will be writing poems. But, before you start, try the following series of activities which will enable you to better understand how poems are written.

Step One: Prewriting

In order to take the mystery out of writing poetry, you need first to understand what lyric poetry is and how a poet goes about creating poems. Let's begin with four key elements that can be found in poetry: imagery, structure, rhythm, and figurative language.

Activity One: Imagery

Sensory images are words and phrases that appeal to our senses of seeing, hearing, touching, smelling, and tasting. Think of sensory images as word pictures. Imagine that you are a photojournalist working for a famous magazine. Your editor assigns you to create a photo study of your neighborhood or school. Most likely, you would try to capture on film a variety of "moments" that show the feeling—the essence—of the place. You might take pictures of:

- two students whispering in class
- a student with a backpack walking along the sidewalk
- a custodian cleaning up a littered cafeteria
- a teacher drinking coffee in the faculty lounge
- cheerleaders practicing in the gym
- the competitors at an athletic event
- a student in the library

Each of these pictures presents in some small way an impression. A poetic image uses language rather than film to create a picture for the mind. Notice, for example, how a poet named Roland Flint recreates the dry, dusty summers of his youth in his poem "August from My Desk":

...I am drifting back to North Dakota
where butterflies are all gone brown with wheat dust.

Now, imagine that you are writing your own poem, "Dreaming of Summer." Try to create your own poetic images—your own word pictures—for the season. What images would you include? The sight of water sparkling in sunshine? The feel of the water when you first jump in? The sounds of a bat hitting a baseball? The smell of hot dogs on a grill? The taste of ice cream? In your notebook, create five images you could use later in a poem about summer.

Activity Two: Analyzing Structure

Poems, unlike narratives and short stories, are written in **lines**, and sometimes **stanzas**, rather than sentences and paragraphs. Some poems, like sonnets and limericks, follow a strict, set format. But in other poems, poets experiment with the form to create certain effects. This style of poetry is called **free verse**. In free verse, poets use the sound of the language to determine when line and stanza breaks should occur.

The paragraph below consists of the first parts of John Tobias's poem, "Reflections on a Gift of Watermelon Pickle Received from a Friend Called Felicity." Tobias originally organized his images in two stanzas—the first consisting of fifteen lines and the second consisting of five lines. Read the images twice. Then, trusting the sound of the language that you hear in your mind, rewrite the paragraph as two stanzas—one of fifteen lines and one of five lines. See how close you come to the poet's original structure.

During that summer when unicorns were still possible; when the purpose of knees was to be skinned; when shiny horsechestnuts (hollowed out fitted with straws crammed with tobacco stolen from butts in family ashtrays) were puffed in green lizard silence while straddling thick branches far above and away from the softening effects of civilization; during that summer— which may never have been at all; but which has become more real than the one that was—watermelons ruled.

Here is Tobias's original version of the first two stanzas of the poem:

During that summer
When unicorns were still possible;
When the purpose of knees
Was to be skinned;
When shiny horsechestnuts
    (Hollowed out
     Fitted with straws
     Crammed with tobacco
     Stolen from butts
     In family ashtrays)
Were puffed in green lizard silence
While straddling thick branches
Far above and away
From the softening effects
Of civilization;

During that summer—
Which may never have been at all;
But which has become more real
Than the one that was—
Watermelons ruled.

Which lines of yours are the same as his? What do you think enabled you to recreate so many of the poet's original lines?

Activity Three: Discerning Rhythm

When composing a melody, a musician uses notes, timing, and arrangement to create a desired rhythm. By carefully selecting and arranging words, a poet also establishes an effective rhythm for a poem. In traditional verse, poets use a fixed rhyme scheme and a set pattern of syllables to establish a constant rhythm. In free verse, poets experiment with a loose rather than a fixed pattern, and they tend to avoid rhyming.

One type of poem with a fixed rhythm and rhyme scheme is the **limerick**. The limerick is a humorous, rhyming poem of five lines. The first, second, and fifth lines of a limerick rhyme and have three feet (repeating rhythmic patterns). The third and fourth lines rhyme and have two feet. To help you pick up the rhythm, try tapping your pen or pencil as you read this limerick. Also, notice the AABBA rhyme scheme.

There was a young woman named *Bright* (A)
Whose speed was much faster than *light*. (A)
She set out one *day* (B)
In a relative *way* (B)
And returned on the previous *night*. (A)

Now, listen to the rhythm as you say the poem again (da = short beat; dum = stressed beat). Here is the beat:

da dum da/ da dum da /da dum (3 feet)
da dum da /da dum da /da dum (3 feet)
da dum da /da dum (2 feet)
da dum da /da dum (2 feet)
da dum da /da dum da /da dum (3 feet)

One tip for writing rhyming verse: before you write additional lines, think of a number of rhyming words from which you have to choose. For instance, after writing this first line of a limerick:

There was a young girl named Claudine...

Think of lots of words that rhyme with *Claudine—teen, mean, lean, green, scene, seen, keen, clean, green, sheen, queen, gasoline, chlorine, machine, praline,* and so forth.

Now, on a separate sheet of paper, write three different second lines for the limerick about Claudine. Try to make the rhythm exactly like the first line.

Next, choose the best of those three lines. Complete the limerick using that line. Be sure to shorten the third and fourth lines. Make those short lines rhyme with each other.

There was a young girl named Claudine.

_____

_____

_____

_____

Finally, in order to practice both rhythm and rhyme in poetry, try two limericks of your own. In case you get stuck, here are a couple of possibilities for first lines. *There was a young boy (girl) from New York* and *There once was a boy (girl) named* _____ (fill in a friend's name). Write the limericks in your notebook.

Activity Four: Understanding Figurative Language

A **figure of speech** is any word or phrase that says one thing and means something more. We all use figures of speech every day. When, for instance, your friend says that her little brother is a "pig" because he eats cheeseburgers without bothering to chew, she is using figurative language. She doesn't mean that he is literally a pig, but rather that he eats like one. She is taking two things that are basically not alike—a boy and a pig—and making the point that, in one way, they *are* alike.

In poetry, figurative language used well can help the reader imagine the picture quickly and clearly. Figures of speech can also make the poem more vivid and emotionally powerful. The writer, for example, describes girls laughing at her by saying, "The giggles hung in the air like melting clouds that were waiting to rain on me." Because of figurative language, you know right away how the laughter made her feel.

In order to learn to use figurative language effectively in poetry and in your other writing, you need to practice different kinds of figures of speech. The two most common figures of speech are **similes** and **metaphors**. Both compare things that don't seem to be alike. A **simile** is a stated comparison, usually using *like* or *as*. William Shakespeare's statement, "Glory is like a circle in the water," is a simile. A **metaphor** is an implied comparison. Shakespeare's statement, "All the world's a stage, and all the men and women merely players," is a metaphor.

Practice making similes and metaphors by finishing each of the following sentences:

1. Rain on a roof sounds like...

_____

2. A backyard barbecue smells like...

_____

3. Ice cream on a hot day tastes like...

_____

4. Jumping into cold water feels like...

_____

Now, practice making metaphors:

1. Summer is...

_____

2. The sun is...

_____

3. Dawn is...

_____

4. Midnight is...

_____

Other figures of speech commonly used in poetry
include **personification**, **paradox**, and **hyperbole**.
We'll take a moment to provide an example of
each one.

Personification gives human qualities to an animal,
thing, or idea. Phrases like "Mother Nature" or "Old
Man Winter" are examples of personification. Robert
Frost provides a startling example of personification in
these lines from his poem "The Secret Sits":

We dance around in a ring and suppose,
But the Secret sits in the middle and knows.

Write examples of personification for each of the
following phrases:

1. The cat is (clever)...

_____

2. The tree is (old)...

_____

3. The sky is (clear)...

_____

4. The car is (fast)...

_____

Paradox is an apparent contradiction that is somehow true on a deeper level. Paradox works especially well when you intend to astonish the reader. Mark Twain, for example, said, "It takes a heap of sense to write good nonsense." And a witty modern writer, Gore Vidal, noted that, "A good deed never goes unpunished."

Now, write examples of paradox for each of the following phrases:

1. She is (beautiful)...

_____

2. The night is (cold)...

_____

3. The day is (cloudy)...

_____

4. The game is (very close)...

_____

Hyperbole is deliberate overstatement, an exaggeration to emphasize truth. Hyperboles like "forever and a day" and "in the middle of nowhere" are not meant to be taken literally. They exaggerate to make a point. This hyperbole by Gene Fowler makes a clear point about writing that you will understand when you start to create poems: "Writing is easy. All you do is stare at a blank sheet of paper until drops of blood form on your forehead."

Write hyperboles for each of the following phrases:

1. He is (big)...

_____

2. The teacher is (smart)...

_____

3. The test is (easy)...

_____

4. The game is (very close)...

_____

Poets often mix together figures of speech. They blend simile, metaphor, personification, paradox, and hyperbole to create symbols. A **symbol** is a figure of speech that takes on central importance in a poem. Symbols give poems and every other kind of writing a deeper meaning, a meaning beyond what the words literally say.

Writing Poems

A poem, though, is more than a collection of techniques. Poems are inward expressions of feelings—something a writer feels deeply. Perhaps it is best simply if we let you read what some famous poets have said about writing poems. In your notebook, write the most interesting quote.

…the definition of a poet: someone who notices and is enormously taken by things that somebody else would walk by. The major thing for a writer to do is develop some means of selecting the best of his memories and ideas and images and to build on them.
—James Dickey

Poetry is life distilled.
—Gwendolyn Brooks

And yet all the time and in spite of the changes in the world—the rapid and incoherent changes—the question at the center, the poet's question, remains the same: Who am I?
—Archibald MacLeish

Poetry is a way of taking life by the throat.
—Robert Frost

If I read a book and it makes my whole body so cold no fire can ever warm me, I know that is poetry. If I feel physically as if the top of my head were taken off, I know that is poetry.
—Emily Dickinson

Poetry springs from something deeper; it's beyond intelligence.
—Jorge Luis Borges

Almost the whole problem of writing poetry is to bring it back to what you feel.
—Robert Lowell

I look at a poem as a performance. I look at the poet as being a man of prowess, just like an athlete.
—Robert Frost

Exploring Ideas

Before we begin with a series of "springboards"—
poem starters for you to use as you build your
understanding of poetry—we will guide you through a
process for writing poems. We've chosen "your school"
as the example since school is an experience everyone
shares. If you don't want to write a poem about your
school, write about your favorite sport or activity.

1. In your notebook, jot down a series of thoughts and
observations about your school. Take a look around.
What are people doing? What do they look like? What
do they remind you of? In May, a typical teacher might,
for example, jot these notes:

—warm, balmy weather
     easily distracted student
     open windows, noise, spring breezes

—prom time
     corsages and tuxedos
     souvenir balloons floating past windows
     voices outside, laughing, singing
     frisbees floating by

—teachers lecturing
     bored students
     frustration

—contrast of lecture and outdoors
     students interested in spring
     not the subject of discussion

2. Now, turn your thoughts and observations into images. Then, make connections between them. Consider ideas you might pursue in the poem. Using the teacher's images presented above, for instance, the writer might decide that both the balloons and the frisbees are floating while the teacher's lecture is sinking fast. This could provide a good contrast for a poem.

Step Two: Composing

Now, take another close look at your notes. Arrange the most interesting images in lines. Work on making the language as vivid as possible. Remember the best words recreate impressions rather than merely <u>talk</u> about them. Experiment with words, lines, maybe even stanzas. Here is a sample draft composed from the thoughts and ideas presented on the previous page:

A Teacher's Springtime

Spinning frisbees
and floating prom balloons
in the courtyard outside—
my students divest themselves of me.
I talk with them still,
but my words neither
spin nor fly.
The beauty of language
of art
dies before them
while they live.

Now, in your notebook, turn your own images into a draft of a poem.

Step Three: Revising

In order to transform your draft into a finished poem, edit the lines and images you have created. Consider these six aspects of good poetry:

Imagery
- Are the images clear and interesting?
- What sensory images should be added or removed?

Condensing Language
- Poetic language is meant to be powerful. Unnecessary words weaken poems. What excess words should be eliminated?

Word Choice
- Are the right words being used in every line?
- Are the nouns and verbs specific and descriptive?
- Look at each word individually and decide if it should be kept, changed, or omitted.

Structure
- Read the poem aloud to hear if the line breaks and stanza breaks sound natural. Try other alternatives. Experiment.

Rhythm
- Read your poem aloud again. How does it sound?
- Rearrange any sections that sound awkward.

Meaning

- What is the central idea that the poem presents?
- Is that central idea stated or implied so that the readers will be able to arrive at some understanding of the poem?

Finalizing the Draft

Go over your poem once again. Make sure the language is clear, concise, and vivid. Write a final, public draft that can be shared with other people.

Here is the final product of the poetic draft presented earlier. Note the changes in imagery, word choice, structure, rhythm, and meaning.

A Teacher's Lament in Springtime

Spinning frisbees
and floating prom balloons
through orchids and apple trees
in the courtyard—
my students divest themselves of me.
My words no longer spin for them
or float
The beauty of language,
of art,
wilts as they bloom:
A seasonal conflict.

Soon they will be fully abloom,
fully blossomed;
while my words will have withered,
shriveled to nothing.

Here is Sara Kirkpatrick's poem, "Mountain Splendor."
Study it to reinforce your understanding of the key
elements of poetry. On the pages following Sara's
poem, six springboards are presented. Each of the
springboards will provide you with opportunities to
create vivid images and vibrant figures of speech.
Organize those images into lines and stanzas, and edit
the poetic drafts to improve imagery, structure, word
choice, and meaning.

Mountain Splendor

I,
the mountain,
protect my vast lands
and guard my sacred earth.
With majesty and royal splendor,
I spread out my lavish robes. They
are adorned with gifts of nature—tall
stately pines, crimson berries, and flowers
with silky leaves and fragile stems. A glassy stem
of beaded water, accented with rich, lacy white foam
is strung about my elegant rifts and rills, leading
to distant valleys beyond. Here I stand in radiant
grandeur, answering only to the burning sun.

Sara Kirkpatrick

Poetic Springboard A

The **haiku** is a short, unrhymed poem that originated in Japan. To create a haiku, write three lines that total approximately 17 syllables. If possible, use lines of 5, 7, and 5 syllables. Use verbs in the present tense.

Since haiku is such a compact poetic form, choose every word *very* carefully. Although haiku are traditionally nature poems, feel free to write about other topics like everyday life, sports, and friends. Here are three good examples of haiku written by young writers.

Silver in the light
A leaf dances in the wind
Dreaming summer dreams

—Sara Kirkpatrick

Long strings of ivy
quietly stretch their fingers
reaching for the peak

—Amanda Jane Elliot

Beauty is unseen,
In a clear blue river stream,
fish hidden beneath.

—Jason Hallstrom

Write your own haiku in your notebook. Write about what this day looks like to you. Be sure that you choose every word carefully.

Now, try another haiku about your favorite sport or activity outdoors. Next, try other haiku about topics of your choice.

Poetic Springboard B

1. Write a poem starting with "I, the ocean" or "I, the wind" or some other nonhuman element. Become that element. Speak in the poem as if you are the ocean or the wind. Write out your images in your notebook.

2. Arrange your images into the lines of a poem.

3. Edit your lines to improve imagery, structure, word choice, and meaning. Rewrite the poem on a separate sheet of paper.

Poetic Springboard C

1. Write a poem talking to something or someone you don't ordinarily talk to: the sun, your favorite actor or singer, your brain, your feet, your bicycle, a politician, anyone or anything that interests you. Write out your images in your notebook.

2. Arrange your images into the lines of a poem.

3. Edit your lines to improve imagery, structure, word choice, and meaning. Rewrite the poem on a separate sheet of paper.

Poetic Springboard D

1. Write down a collection of thoughts and observations about any group that interests you: athletes, eighth-grade boys (girls), bus drivers, movie stars, joggers, sisters, brothers, parents, etc. Write out your images.
2. Select your best images and arrange them into the lines of a poem.
3. Edit your lines to improve imagery, structure, word choice, and meaning. Rewrite the poem on a separate sheet of paper.

Poetic Springboard E

1. Write down a number of images that begin with a particular color ("Blue is…" or "Red is…"). Consider using colors such as tan, aqua, gray, rose, gold, silver. Write out your images in your notebook.
2. Select your best images and arrange them into the lines of a "color poem."
3. Edit your lines to improve imagery, structure, word choice, and meaning. Rewrite the poem on a separate sheet of paper.

Poetic Springboard F

Take a highly abstract word (such as *happiness, loneliness, success, freedom,* etc.). Write down a number of sensory images that it brings to mind. For example,

Loneliness is
A stick floating down the river
with no one watching
A tree...

Now, follow these steps:

1. Write your sensory images in your notebook.
2. Arrange your images into the lines of a poem.
3. Edit your lines to improve imagery, structure, word choice, and meaning. Rewrite the poem on a separate sheet of paper.

Completing Poetry Responses

Ask a peer editor to read through your poems and choose the three he or she likes best. Have the editor answer these questions about each of the poems.

1. What is the poem about?
2. List two images that you liked.
3. Is there an image or two that confused you?
4. Suggest four word changes. Make the words more specific and vivid.
5. What changes in line and stanza breaks would you recommend?

Writing the Final Draft

Choose two of the three poems your editor evaluated. Make these two poems perfect. Improve the poems' imagery, structure, rhythm, figurative language, and meaning. Read your editor's comments again. Make the language specific and vivid. Check every word. Go back over the poems as often as you need to. The poet James Dickey, for example, said, "How many drafts I write depends on the poem. With a longer one like 'The Firebombing,' I'd say certainly 150-175, because you are searching for some kind of order...Then you are also trying to render it unforgettable." When you have rendered your poems unforgettable, write final, public copies of them to be shared with other people.

Proofreading

After reworking your poems a number of times, go over them one last time to correct errors in style and usage. Even though poets are allowed "poetic license"—the chance to break rules of grammar and usage deliberately in order to create an effect in a poem—you need to proofread the final copy of each of your poems to make sure that the effects you want are clear for your readers.

The Writer's Supplement

Before you finish any piece of writing, you need to proofread it in order to insure that you have corrected errors in English style and usage. You may not catch every error, but try to make sure that every finished piece of writing is reasonably free from errors.

We will not, of course, review all of the rules of English style and usage here, but we will provide ten important guidelines that will enable you to focus your proofreading and eliminate common errors that confuse readers. The first five focus on style, and the second five focus on usage.

Ten Guidelines for Good Writing

1) Be clear. All public writing is an attempt to communicate with other people. Your readers need to be able to understand what you are saying. If a sentence or paragraph confuses you, your readers will certainly be confused as well.

2) Use the active voice. The active voice (*Andre hit the ball*) is more clear and direct than the passive (*The ball was hit by Andre*). Wherever possible, change the passive voice to the active.

3) Cut unnecessary words. Get rid of repetitive words and phrases. In the sentence, *The coach yelled and screamed at the players,* the words *yelled* and *screamed* are redundant. Cut one of the words.

4) Use the right words. Remember that your writing is an attempt to communicate with other people. Make sure you use words that others will understand. *Sally was a loquacious, indeed verbose, individual with a propensity toward excessive verbiage* is not nearly as effective as *Sally was a chatterbox.*

5) Combine choppy sentences. Combining sentences enables you to make your writing smoother. You will also be able to say what you want in fewer words. The exercises on the following pages will give you the opportunity to practice combining sentences and to hone your skills related to the other nine guidelines.

6) Do not confuse similar words. Here is a list of word pairs that are often misused. Note the difference in meaning between the words in each pair.

Accept and *except*
I can't *accept* (admit to) the notion that only men can be soldiers.
Everyone went to dinner *except* (but) Paul.

Affect and *effect*
Bobby was deeply *affected* (influenced) by his older brother's speech.
What was the *effect* (result) of the flood in Youngstown?

already and *all ready*
Sybil had *already* (by this time) returned from Ireland when the airline strike began.
Are you *all ready* (everyone set) to go to the concert?

altogether and *all together*

The judge was not *altogether* (entirely) impressed with the defendent's plea.

Are the members of the group *all together* (everyone gathered)?

among and *between*

Among (more than two) the ten of us, we must have one person who can spell.

Between (two) the two of us, we must have enough money to pay the bill.

bring and *take*

Bring (to) the newspaper here, please.

Take (away) the dirty clothes to the laundromat.

farther and *further*

George can run *farther* (distance) than Reggie can.

The *further* (time) we discussed the issue, the angrier we became.

fewer and *less*

Fewer (with numerical amounts) pencils than we expected were left after the exam.

The new law did *less* (with abstract quantitties) than we had anticipated.

imply and *infer*

Without actually saying so, the waiter *implied* (suggested) that I order a different meal.

I *inferred* (concluded) from his outfit that he had spent a month in the woods.

number and *amount*

A significant *number* (a quantity composed of equal units) of people rejected the mayor's idea.

A large *amount* (total) of snow fell in the fields last night.

7) Avoid fragments and run-on sentences. A sentence fragment is a group of words that does not present a complete thought. A run-on sentence includes two or more sentences joined incorrectly. A fragment can be corrected:

• by changing an inappropriate verb or adding a missing verb.

Incorrect: Hector running to the bakery.
Correct: Hector was running to the bakery.
Or: Hector ran to the bakery.

• by adding a missing subject.

Incorrect: Was governing with dignity.
Correct: The older leader was governing with dignity.

• by adding a missing subject or verb.

Incorrect: To go on vacation tomorrow.
Correct: Steve decided to go on vacation tomorrow.

A run-on can be eliminated:
• by adding an appropriate period and a capital letter.
Incorrect: Marcia plays beautifully, the audience cheers.
Correct: Marcia plays beautifully. The audience cheers.

• by adding a subordinating conjunction.
Incorrect: Marcia plays beautifully, the audience cheers.
Correct: When Marcia plays beautifully, the audience cheers.

8) Match subjects and verbs. A singular verb must be used with a singular subject, and a plural verb must be used with a plural subject. Here is a list of four common subject/verb problems to avoid in your writing.

• A singular subject always requires a singular verb, even when the subject is followed by a preposition with a plural object.
Incorrect: Each of the horses *are* running in the race.
Correct: Each of the horses *is* running in the race.

• The following words as subjects require a singular verb: *each, either, neither, one, everyone, every one, no one, anyone, someone, everybody, nobody, anybody, somebody.*
Incorrect: Neither of the teachers *are* in a hurry.
Correct: Neither of the teachers *is* in a hurry.

• The following words are subjects and always require plural verbs: *few, both, many, several.*
Incorrect: Many of us *was* surprised by the speech.
Correct: Many of us *were* surprised by the speech.

• The following words as subjects require singular or plural verbs depending upon the meaning of the sentence: *some, any, all, none, most.*
Incorrect: Some of the players *was* tired.
Correct: Some of the players *were* tired.
Incorrect: Some of the steak *were* eaten.
Correct: Some of the steak *was* eaten.

9) Use adjectives and adverbs correctly. Here is a list of four rules to remember about using adjectives and adverbs.

• Adverbs modify action verbs, adjectives, and other adverbs.
Incorrect: Sam hits the ball *bad*.
Correct: Sam hits the ball *badly*.

• Adjectives rather than adverbs follow *linking* (nonaction) verbs.
Incorrect: The banana smells *badly*.
Correct: The banana smells *bad*.

• The comparative form (Larg*er,* funn*ier,* etc.) of the adjective is used to compare two things.
Incorrect: William is the *biggest* of the two boys.
Correct: William is the *bigger* of the two boys.

• The superlative form (larg*est,* funn*iest,* etc.) is used to compare three or more things.
Incorrect: Of Brooks, Allen, and Cosby, who is the *funnier* comedian?
Correct: Of Brooks, Allen, and Cosby, who is the *funniest* comedian?

10) Spell correctly. Many professional writers have trouble spelling, but they learn to look up words or to find someone to help them correct spelling errors. Many computer word processing programs now include spell checkers. Because nothing bothers readers more than strangely spelled words, find a good way to check your spelling before completing a final draft of any piece of writing.

After you have reviewed these ten guidelines, do the following sentence combining exercises. These exercises will enable you to practice using the guidelines to improve your final drafts.

Sentence Combining I

Here are ten sets of sentences taken from students' narratives. On a separate sheet of paper, combine each of these sets of sentences into one sentence. Remember, there is always more than one good way to combine sentences.

1. My first-grade teacher was Mrs. Whalen. Everybody loved her.

2. It was a Monday in the lazy days of summer. Like every other Monday I was bored.

3. His house was red brick with black shutters. Rusty patio furniture was sitting outside.

4. The minute I turn into the long driveway I fade into my own little world. From then on nothing out of camp matters.

5. We waited until 3:00. At 3:00 we put our bathing suits on, and we ran down to the lake.

6. While we were riding, we saw the class clown of our school, Brent. We saw him talking to his father, who was a policeman.

7. We walked to the path that led to our destination. We quietly walked up the path. Everyone was scared of getting caught.

8. "Bewitched" was a television program. In it was a lady, Samantha, and her daughter, Tabitha. These two females possessed witch powers.

9. To play this game you would need a field. You could use a baseball field, park, or even the street. In my neighborhood we used the street.

10. Those girls played with such style and grace. I wished I could play with them. There was only one problem. I didn't know how.

Sentence Combining II

Here are ten sets of sentences taken from students' narratives. On a separate sheet of paper, combine each of these sets of sentences into one sentence. Remember, there is always more than one good way to combine sentences.

1. It was the first day of school. Pam, my best friend, waited at the bus stop for my arrival.

2. It happened on a very humid Tuesday afternoon. It was in the summer and my friend and I were bored.

3. France is a beautiful place. In some ways it is much like the United States and in others ways it is quite different.

4. It was in my fifth grade gym class. You know, the place where dodgeball and four-square are the big time.

5. There was one incident in grammar school that I recall rather vividly. I believe it was in the second grade.

6. I had made a new best friend. Her name was Betty. She had short curly black hair and black eyes, and her face was kind of oval.

7. It was this summer, the summer of '86, when I took on a new and exciting responsibility. I took a summer job being a camp counselor.

8. We sat down and petted him. At that moment he jerked his head up, straightened his ears and knew something was up.

INDEX

Acknowledgments

Pages 16-19, 40-41, 48, 49 *To Kill a Mockingbird* by Harper Lee, copyright 1960. Reprinted by permission of HarperCollins Publishers.

Pages 58-62 "Breakfast" from *The Long Valley* by John Steinbeck, copyright 1966. Reprinted by permission of Viking Penguin.

Page 106 "August from My Desk" by Roland Flint, copyright 1965. Reprinted by permission of *The Atlantic Monthly Company*.

Pages 107-108 "Reflections on a Gift of Watermelon Pickles from a Friend Called Felicity" by John Tobias, copyright 1989. Reprinted by permission of the author.

Page 113 "The Secret Sits" from *The Poetry of Robert Frost* by Edward Connery Lathem, copyright 1970. Reprinted by permission of Henry Holt and Company, Inc.